Cause of Our Joy

Cause of Our Joy

by Sr. Mary Francis LeBlanc, O. Carm.

BOOKS & MEDIA

BOSTON

Nihil Obstat:
Rt. Rev. Paul M. Fusilier, STD
Censor Librorum

Imprimatur:
+ Most Rev. Maurice Schexnayder
Bishop of Lafayette

Scripture excerpts from *The New American Bible,* © 1970, used herein by permission of the Confraternity of Christian Doctrine, copyright owner.

Library of Congress Catalog Card Number: 74-79803

ISBN 0-8198-1414-8

Printed and published in the U.S.A. by Pauline Books & Media, 50 St. Paul's Avenue, Boston, MA 02130.

http://www.pauline.org

Pauline Books & Media is the publishing house of the Daughters of St. Paul, an international congregation of women religious serving the Church with the communications media.

5 6 7 8 9   02 01 00 99 98

To Mary

Contents

Foreword

From time to time through the centuries, the Blessed Virgin Mary has appeared to devout believers to bring a message of consolation and faith. While a great many apparitions are reported, the Church has officially approved only a small number of these. In doing so, the Church simply states that there is nothing in them that is contrary to the Catholic faith, and that they are worthy of belief. This does not mean, however, that Catholics are required to believe in them, for these apparitions are private revelations. Although not a part of official Catholic teaching, they still can remind us that God sometimes enters our lives in a dramatic way.

This book tells the stories of some of the major apparitions of the Virgin. Some of these concern devotions that have taken deep root among Catholics, such as the rosary, the scapular and the miraculous medal. In others, Mary appears as a tender mother, full of concern and care for us. As she said to Juan Diego, "Let nothing discourage you.... Do not fear any illness or trouble, anxiety or pain. Am I not here who am your Mother? Are you not under my shadow and protection?" May every reader of this book come to personally experience the same love and tenderness of our Blessed Mother.

I

Cause of Our Joy

"Hail, full of grace, the Lord is with thee!"
A celestial greeting for an immaculate maid.
Heaven's message delivered in solemn majesty
To her who was to mother God man made.
The angelic visitor with a "Fiat" laden
Heavenward ascends with haste.
On the earthen floor kneels the trusting maiden,
Love beaming from her enraptured face.
O Cause of Our Joy, did you then know
Of the crib, of the cross, of the Eucharist divine?
Did your Spouse, the Holy Spirit, to you show
What your fiat would mean to all mankind?
Did the lowing cattle and the lowly manger
With the smiling Babe on the hay
Flash before your eyes as a little stranger
Whispers, "'Tis Christmas day"?
Did you know then that your Child divine
Would with Calvary's key open heaven's door?
That he was the Way, the Truth, the Light that would
    shine
Leading men back to God once more?
That so intense would his love for souls be
That he could not leave them alone,
That a Eucharistic miracle of love would be he —
Tabernacled food enthroned?
O Cause of Our Joy, what was your thought
As Gabriel vanished from you?
"'Twas God and his will that filled your heart
For he was your sufficiency true."

Mary is truly the "Cause of Our Joy." By giving her consent to God's request, Mary has been the cause of humanity's obtaining the joys of heaven again because she gave us our divine Redeemer. Jesus, of course, is the direct cause, for by his voluntary death on the cross, he opened the gates of heaven. By his life on earth, he has shown us how to get to heaven. He is the Truth, the Life, and the Way. He is Mary's Babe, Mary's Boy, Mary's Son. She gave him to us. She knew *what* she gave and *why* she gave. In accord with God's will, she willed to be the Mother of the Redeemer, and she knew what that meant.

Knowing this, how was Mary able to utter her "Fiat" with so much sincerity, with so much love and with so much self-forgetfulness and trust? The answer is found in Mary's life story.

Where Mary was born is not exactly known. Some authors say in Jerusalem; others say in Nazareth. It is believed that her father was Joachim, of the royal house of David, and that her mother was Anne, of the priestly family of Aaron. An ancient tradition tells us that Joachim and Anne had been married many years but had had no children. They grieved greatly over this. They loved God and longed to please him in every way possible. They knew and loved Holy Scripture. Like every good, holy Jewish couple, they longed for the coming of the Messiah. They hoped to have him among their descendants if God so chose to bless them. They promised God to consecrate their firstborn to him. Their prayers and their holy living continually stormed heaven for them. Finally, God worked a miracle of love and blessed them with a baby girl. The name Mary or Miriam means lady or mistress.

Mary brought much joy to her father and mother. Like any little baby, she learned to coo and to laugh, to prattle and to sing. Her loving parents taught her to talk, to walk, and to pray. Many believe that even as a tiny child she understood well that her parents had vowed her to God. She had learned from the cradle to love God. When she was three years old, tradition relates, she joyfully went to the temple in Jerusalem with her father and mother to consecrate herself to God. Her holy parents presented her to the priest in charge, and he presented her to God. It is believed by some that Mary remained in the temple until she was twelve years old. Others believe that she returned home and was educated by her mother.

In the temple or at home, Mary learned to read and to write. She learned to sew and to embroider. She learned to cook and to manage a house, to pray and to sing. Daily Mary grew closer to God, corresponding with the many graces he lavished upon her. Grace prompted her to make a vow of virginity, something unknown to the Jews. She knew of the coming of the Messiah from her study of Holy Scripture. She knew, too, that the time of his coming was close at hand. Devoutly she prayed that it would be soon. It is believed that she prayed also to be worthy to become the little handmaid of the Mother of the Savior. In her humility she longed to serve her who would mother the Messiah.

When Mary had reached the customary marriageable age among the Jews, her relatives insisted that she marry. Since she was an only child, the law obliged it. Mary trusted divine Providence. She felt that God had willed her vow of virginity, and that now he was willing her marriage. She knew that God would take care of her.

The partner God chose for her was one truly capable of understanding her. Joseph, the carpenter of Nazareth, was, like Mary, of the house of David. He agreed to lead a pure life within the bonds of marriage. Joseph was holy, just, humble, loving and upright. He

loved God fervently. He, too, longed for the coming of
the Messiah. He, too, knew and loved Holy Scripture. He
understood Mary. With one mind and one heart they
agreed to fulfill the will of God together. The espousal
ceremony was joyously celebrated. According to custom,
the two resided in their respective homes in Nazareth
until the marriage ceremony about a year later.

During this time God sent the angel Gabriel to the
priest Zechariah in Jerusalem. Zechariah had married
Mary's cousin Elizabeth many years before. Their great
sorrow was that they had no children.

God blessed their holiness and their prayers. The
angel of the Lord appeared while Zechariah was offering
incense in the temple. The angel announced the birth of a
little son. Astonished, Zechariah could not understand
how this could be, since he and his wife were both so old.
Because he doubted the angel's words, Zechariah was
struck dumb until what had been announced would take
place.

Six months later, the same angel, Gabriel, was sent
to Mary. St. Luke gives this account:

"In the sixth month, the angel Gabriel was sent
from God to a town of Galilee named Nazareth, to a
virgin betrothed to a man named Joseph, of the house of
David. The virgin's name was Mary. Upon arriving, the
angel said to her: 'Rejoice, O highly favored daughter!
The Lord is with you. Blessed are you among women.'
She was deeply troubled by his words, and wondered
what his greeting meant. The angel went on to say to
her: 'Do not fear, Mary. You have found favor with God.
You shall conceive and bear a son and give him the name
Jesus. Great will be his dignity and he will be called Son
of the Most High. The Lord God will give him the throne
of David his father. He will rule over the house of Jacob
forever and his reign will be without end.'

"Mary said to the angel, 'How can this be since I do not know man?' The angel answered her: 'The Holy Spirit will come upon you and the power of the Most High will overshadow you; hence, the holy offspring to be born will be called Son of God. Know that Elizabeth your kinswoman has conceived a son in her old age; she who was thought to be sterile is now in her sixth month, for nothing is impossible with God.'

"Mary said: 'I am the servant of the Lord. Let it be done to me as you say.' With that the angel left her" (Lk 1:26-38).

As the angel disappeared, Mary pondered the will of God. She understood that by a miracle she was going to be at once virgin and mother. As mother of the Messiah she would cooperate in the redemption of the human race. Mary then thought of her cousin Elizabeth. How happy she was for her! Mary longed to rejoice with her.

Mary joined a caravan heading for Jerusalem. In the spirit of loving charity, she went to visit her cousin. It was probably springtime. With love and joy, Mary must have taken note of the beauties of nature as they traveled. Humbly she praised God.

Elizabeth's home was very near Jerusalem. What joy Mary brought to Elizabeth with her surprise visit! Mary remained with Elizabeth until the birth of her little son, John the Baptizer. She then returned to her own home in Nazareth to await her marriage ceremony.

Mary joyfully greeted Joseph, who was happy to see her again. But as time went by Joseph became puzzled about Mary. He did not know about the Incarnation. Finally, God sent an angel to reveal it to him in a dream. St. Matthew tells us that the angel said to Joseph, "Joseph, son of David, have no fear about taking Mary as your wife. It is by the Holy Spirit that she has conceived this child. She is to have a son and you are to name him Jesus because he will save his people from their sins" (Mt 1:20-21). Joseph loved and trusted Mary. Now that he knew her secret he could help her prepare for the coming great event.

The wedding ceremony took place with the usual festive solemnity. Then Joseph happily brought his young wife home. Mary went about her housework cheerfully and prayerfully. She went to the well for water, prepared her husband's meals, cleaned her little house, and after spending some time in prayer, joyfully wove cloth. With the cloth she made precious baby clothes as well as clothes for Joseph and herself. How happy she was when Joseph surprised her with a tiny baby's crib! Together she and Joseph waited and prayed, drawing closer to God.

Since it was a part of the vast Roman Empire, Palestine was under Roman rule at that time. Caesar Augustus, the Roman Emperor, ordered a census to be taken of all his subjects. He wanted to know how many people he governed. Joseph and Mary who were of the house and family of David, had to register in Bethlehem, the town of David. Bethlehem, a little to the south of Jerusalem, was many miles away from Nazareth. It was about seven days' travel. Joseph felt very upset that Mary should have to make such a long journey in the cold weather. Mary calmly told Joseph not to worry. She told him that God was shaping everything according to his own designs, that the circumstances were simply the work of divine Providence and that God would care for them.

Mary cheerfully mounted the little donkey Joseph provided for her. Taking only the bare necessities with them, Mary and Joseph traveled to Bethlehem. Mary recalled the trip she had taken in the early spring. She was following the same route, but now all was so different under the mighty grasp of winter. Joseph was worried about her. In her gentle, sweet way, Mary tried to make light of the discomforts of travel. There was still so much beauty all around—the sky, the mountains in the distance, the villages they passed, the sheep on the hills. God seemed so near to them.

As they approached Bethlehem toward nightfall, Joseph's anxiety increased. He knew no one in the town. So many people had come to Bethlehem for the same reason that he had come. The inns were overcrowded. He tried in vain to find shelter at private homes. No one had room that night. But on the outskirts of the town was a stable which could give them adequate protection for the night.

Joseph helped Mary to dismount and fixed her a nice bed of hay. The lone cow nearby looked on with big, friendly eyes. The little donkey contentedly ate some hay and drank the cool water Joseph provided. Joseph quietly went to check outside. He looked at the beautiful stars overhead. Softly he whispered a prayer that God would help them find a house on the morrow. All was peaceful and quiet. Joseph went back into the stable.

The soft light of Joseph's lantern enveloped Mary, who was sitting on the hay holding a tiny bundle. She called Joseph softly. In awe Joseph realized whom she was holding. Reverently he fell to his knees. After a while he looked around and found a manger used for feeding the cattle. He lined it with hay. Mary gently placed the little Babe in the manger. She and Joseph knelt beside him, the first adorers.

How long he remained kneeling in loving contemplation Joseph did not know, but voices outside aroused him. Quickly he went to the door. Shepherds stood there, begging to come in to adore Christ, the Savior. In astonishment, Joseph stepped aside to let them enter. They humbly knelt and adored their Infant God.

The shepherds told Mary and Joseph that an angel of the Lord had appeared to them as they were tending their flock. The angel had told them the good news of great joy that in the town of David their Savior had been born. As a sign he had said that they would find an infant wrapped in swaddling clothes and lying in a manger. Then a multitude of angels had appeared praising God and saying, "Glory to God in high heaven, peace on earth to those on whom his favor rests" (Lk 2:14). The angels had disappeared and the shepherds had come quickly to find the Child. Kneeling there in humble adoration, they understood the angel's message. They returned to their flock glorifying and praising God.

Joseph was able to find a house for Mary and the Infant. Perhaps the shepherds were instrumental. According to law, on the eighth day the child was circumcised and given the name Jesus. Desiring to fulfill the law in all things, Mary and Joseph presented the Child Jesus in the temple at Jerusalem forty days after his birth. They bought him back for five shekels. Two turtle doves were presented as a purification offering.

Meanwhile, a holy old man, inspired by the Holy Spirit, entered the temple. It had been revealed to him by the Holy Spirit that he would see Christ before he would die. When he saw the Baby in Mary's arms, he asked to hold him. He received Jesus with joy, praising God. He blessed Mary and Joseph and told Mary that the Child was destined for the rise and fall of many in Israel, but that her own soul would be pierced by a sword.

A very old lady, the prophetess Anna, entered at the same time. She saw Mary, Joseph and the Infant. Inspired by God, she recognized her Savior. She began to praise God and to speak of the redemption of Israel. With joy, Mary stored all this in her heart.

One day while Mary was singing a soft lullaby to her little Son, she heard a loud knock on the door. Joseph, who had been working in the back room, quickly answered it. Three men in strange and costly robes entered. At the sight of Mary and the Infant, they prostrated themselves with joy, offering their treasures, the most precious in their countries: gold, frankincense and myrrh.

They told Mary and Joseph how they, as astrologers, had seen the star which was to herald the birth of the Messiah. They had followed the star as far as Jerusalem, where they had lost sight of it. On inquiry from Herod, the king, they had been told by the priests and scribes that according to prophecy the Messiah was to be born in Bethlehem. Herod had requested that the astrologers return to him after they had found the newborn King of Israel so that Herod, too, could pay his respects. The magi were warned in a dream not to return to Herod; so they went back to their own countries by another way.

An angel appeared in a dream to Joseph and told him to take the Child and his mother to Egypt and to remain there until told to return, for wicked Herod planned to harm the Child. Joseph, Mary and Jesus immediately departed for Egypt. Meanwhile the heartless king, seeing that he had been tricked by the magi, put to death every baby boy in Bethlehem who was two years old or under. These little martyrs were the first to shed their innocent blood for Christ.

Some say the Holy Family remained in Egypt only a few months. Others say that they stayed there a few years. Herod did not live very long after he had martyred the holy innocents. After he was dead, an angel of the Lord appeared to Joseph and told him that it was safe to return to Israel. Fearing Herod's son, Joseph did not go to Judea. Instead, he took Mary and Jesus to Nazareth, in the region of Galilee.

In Nazareth, like any happy child, Jesus continued to grow under the loving care of his mother. Mary was his first teacher. What a joy it was for Joseph to show his little foster-Child how to use the hammer, how to hold the saw, and to explain what a nail was for. What happiness and joy the three shared in the holy house at Nazareth. Peace, contentment, love and union with God reigned in that humble house. Jesus lovingly helped his mother to get water from the well, to sweep the floor, and so forth. As he grew older, he cheerfully helped Joseph with his carpentry.

Every year the Holy Family went to Jerusalem at the feast of the Passover. When Jesus was twelve years old, they went to the Temple according to custom. They remained in Jerusalem until the end of the week's ceremonies. The pilgrims customarily formed long caravans and traveled without definite order. The men generally traveled together, and the women formed a separate group. Jesus had remained in the Temple unknown to his parents. Joseph thought he was with Mary, and Mary thought he was with Joseph.

When they had gone about a day's journey and stopped to rest, Mary and Joseph could not find Jesus. They rushed back to Jerusalem and began a careful, heartbreaking search. On the third day they found him in the Temple, sitting in the midst of the doctors and scribes, listening to them and asking questions. Mary called to him and told him of their sorrow at not having found him. He returned to Nazareth with them, growing in wisdom and grace before God and everyone.

Like Joseph, Jesus became a carpenter, making and repairing objects of wood. Exteriorly the Holy Family was much like any other humble Jewish family. But the interior recollection, the life of union with God, the life of prayer and love within the little household radiated joy.

Joseph, the provider, the guardian of Mary, the foster father of Jesus, grew in holiness in the company of earth's holiest.

It is believed that when Jesus was a young man, God called Joseph home. Joseph is truly the patron of a happy death, for at his deathbed knelt Mary, his pure and chaste spouse, the Mother of God. She had ever been a loving and devoted wife. Jesus, the Author of life and death, stood beside him, speaking words of courage, love and sympathy. With Jesus' tender smile upon him and Mary's loving gaze, Joseph bade farewell to the two for whom he had lived. What joy to stand before God to give an account of his stewardship! Jesus tenderly consoled his mother. Joseph had been so good to both of them.

Jesus continued his carpenter's task until he was about thirty years old. Joy and sorrow mingled in Mary's heart when at last he came to tell her he must leave for his public ministry. She knew the prophecies. What he would have to suffer! Yet what glory he would give to God, his Father! He would repair the honor of God; he would save his people. He would reopen the gates of heaven. He would give to the world the means of sanctification. How many would accept his teachings? How many would accept the means of sanctification? Her mother's heart and mother's love followed his every move.

The first public miracle worked by Jesus was at the request of his mother. Jesus and his disciples had been invited to a wedding feast at Cana. Mary was there also. Mary saw that the wine was running short. In order to prevent embarrassment for the bride and the groom, she told Jesus. Jesus disclosed his power and glory by turning water into wine. His disciples believed in him.

It is believed that during our Lord's public life Mary remained for the most part at Nazareth, leading a secluded life of prayer. But her heart was with her Son. What joy to get news of him, a short visit from him, to know that all was well! How her heart ached when she realized how much hatred was being stirred up against her Son. So few really knew and understood him; even her own relatives had not understood. But Mary courageously stood by.

Mary was in Jerusalem for Jesus' last Passover on earth. She, too, made the "Way of the Cross." When she met her Son for a fleeting moment, it was to bolster courage. Mary stood at the foot of the cross, one with the victim. Her heart bled for her Son and her God. Her heart bled for her children—they knew not what they had done. She accepted them from her dying Son in the person of John, the beloved. Her sorrow, her sacrifice was so great that she merited the title Queen of Martyrs. Truly her heart was pierced with the sword of sorrow.

Courageously Mary received her Son's body as he was taken gently down from the cross. How lovingly she held him, her Son, her God, a sacrificial victim for the sins of humanity. As she laid him to rest in the new tomb of Joseph of Arimathea and sealed the door, her heart stayed with him. John led her away. She knew when she had said "yes" to the angel Gabriel that Jesus would have to suffer. What a terrific price she had to pay!

Mary patiently waited. She believed her Son's words. He had foretold this many times. Death was the prelude to life.

What joy was Mary's on that Easter morning as her Son stood before her, resplendent, glorious! His five wounds shone like jewels. How well she understood everything then! How she and Jesus rejoiced! The gates of heaven were reopened, the purchase price for humanity's redemption was paid in full, the acceptable sacrifice of atonement was consummated. People had now but to use the channel of graces prepared for them by Christ, and heaven would be theirs. Joy forever!

Again, Mary's joy was mingled with sadness as her Son bade her farewell on the day he ascended to his Father. His physical presence was no longer with her, but spiritually he was so close. Mary knew that as Mother of the infant Church she had to help nurture it. She was present when the Holy Spirit came down upon the apostles to strengthen them and to fill them with the needed zeal. She watched and prayed and counseled as the Church began to grow, to get strong, and to expand. John, the beloved apostle, cared for her as his true mother.

Mary's consuming love and longing for her divine Son caused him to come for her. It is believed that Mary died several years after Jesus' own death, either in Jerusalem or in Ephesus. Tenderly and reverently, the apostles buried her. But Jesus would not let his Mother's precious, immaculate body remain in the tomb. He had it carried into heaven where it was reunited with her pure soul.

According to tradition, when the apostles opened the coffin, only lilies were found. Knowing how pure and immaculate Mary had always been and how much Jesus had loved her and she him, the Church rightly proclaimed as a dogma of faith Mary's Assumption into heaven. This feast is celebrated on August fifteenth.

In heaven, as Queen of heaven and earth, Mary has continued her role as Mother. Through the ages, her concern, her love, her intercession have benefited mankind. It was her motherly solicitude which gave us the rosary, the scapular, the miraculous medal. It was her motherly solicitude which pleaded for prayer and penance at La Salette, at Lourdes, at Fatima. Because of the many recent recorded miracles, there is belief that Mary has repeatedly visited the world during the nineteenth and twentieth centuries. Should there be any doubt or question concerning her same maternal solicitude in earlier centuries? Only in heaven will we really know how much and how often Mary has played her role of Mother. She is so powerful because she is the Mother of God.

Mary can never be loved too much. To love and honor her does not take anything away from God as some erroneously believe. When we truly love someone, be it mother, friend, sister or brother, we are happy that he or she is loved and honored by others. We rejoice! So, too, does God rejoice. He loves Mary, and he wants her to be loved and honored. In fact, to honor and venerate Mary is to honor God, for in honoring her who mothered Jesus we honor and glorify the Trinity. God the Father is truly the Father of Jesus, whose Mother is Mary. Mary is also the privileged daughter of the Father. Of all creatures, she corresponded with all the graces lavished upon her. God the Father loves Mary dearly and expects us to do likewise. God the Son is truly Mary's Son, substance of her substance. She bore him, fed him, clothed him, and taught him. He loves, obeys and cherishes his Mother. He expects us to do likewise. God, the Holy Spirit, is the Spouse of Mary. In the Apostles' Creed we say, "I believe in God, the Father Almighty, Creator of heaven and earth; and in Jesus Christ, his only Son, our Lord, who was conceived by the Holy Spirit." Mary is also the temple of the Holy Spirit. Because of her fullness of grace, he abides within her in a special way. Mary loves the Trinity. She loves to be called the Lily of the Trinity.

God has been so very good to us. The label "joy" could be applied to so much in our lives, yet our greatest joy, the world's greatest joy, heaven's greatest joy has been and is Jesus. Mary gave us Jesus. The invocation in the litany of the Blessed Virgin "Cause of Our Joy" is truly appropriate. May Mary, the Lily of the Trinity, be ever the "Cause of Our Joy."

II

Our Lady of Lourdes

The strange noise stopped—now there
    wasn't a rustle.
The girl looked around—all was utterly
    still.
Then again the rustle of leaves shouting a
    welcome,
And lo, a light in the niche of the cave in the
    hill,
And, Mary, resplendently Immaculate,
    smiled
As gently she beckoned to her favored
    child.
Ah, Bernadette, you whispered Aves
There at the beautiful Lady's feet.
You gave to the world her requests
For penance, for prayer, for devotion so
    sweet.
You brought the world there
To plead in prayer and in song.
Now the "Ave, Maria"
Resounds all day long
From hearts full of love,
Of gratitude, of pleas.
O confidante of Mary, we too need
A smile from the Lady of the Pyrenees.

For those who know Lourdes, the very word brings to mind a host of welcoming pictures and thoughts. Mary has made it practically a vestibule of heaven.

Lourdes is a small mountain town in southern France, at the foot of the Pyrenees, the beautiful mountains which separate France and Spain. Here in this little town on January 7, 1844, a baby girl came to bring joy to her parents, Francis Soubirous and Louise Casterot. The baby was baptized two days later, receiving the name Marie Bernarde after St. Bernard, who loved our Lady with great devotion. Since her godmother and aunt was also named Bernarde, the baby was called Little Bernarde or Bernadette.

When Bernadette was about six months old, her mother became very ill. She was forced to send her baby to a friend, Marie Aravant, who lived at Bartres, a village about two miles from Lourdes. Mrs. Aravant was a good Christian woman who was grieving over the death of her own baby. She gladly nursed and cared for little Bernadette as though she were her own little girl. After fifteen months Bernadette was taken back home to her parents in Lourdes.

Bernadette's father operated a flour mill. He was not a very good miller. He often sent out flour of poor quality. He was easygoing and not at all thrifty. His wife was very much the same, easygoing and thriftless, but both were good-hearted, God-fearing people. By the time Bernadette was eleven years old, the wolf of poverty was at the door.

Some people owed the miller for work done on credit, but he would not demand his money. Finally, the Soubirous family was forced to leave the mill. They moved from place to place, practically to every part of the town, until Mr. Soubirous, unable to pay any rent, obtained permission from one of his wife's relatives to live in a small building he owned in the Rue de Petits-Fossés. This one-room building had once been the jail of Lourdes.

At this time, when they moved to the old jail, the Soubirous children were Bernadette, the oldest; Antoinette, age nine; Jean Marie, age four; and Justin, just a few months old. Two little brothers had already gone to God, and two more were to come to add to the joy of the household. Though poor, the Soubirous family was devout and happy, close to God and to our Lady through the nightly rosary and faithful attendance at Sunday Mass.

In 1857, Marie Aravant, Bernadette's foster mother, asked Mr. and Mrs. Soubirous to allow Bernadette to live with her at Bartres to help her look after the children. Bernadette went to Bartres but instead of being given care of the children, she was given charge of the sheep. The little shepherdess spent her days on the hillsides caring for the sheep, playing with the lambs, gathering wild flowers, and weaving them into garlands in honor of our Lady. In the quiet and peace of the hills she felt close to God and to our Lady. She kept her rosary with her always, and often during the day she would say it over and over.

Bernadette could neither read nor write. Long before, it had been planned that she would be sent to school at least to learn her catechism, but there was always some work to be done. Time went by, and she had never been sent. Bernadette had not yet made her First Communion. She had such a great longing to do so that Mrs. Aravant decided to try to teach her the catechism herself. But poor Bernadette could remember so little of what she was taught, even after repeating over and over again, that Mrs. Aravant, losing patience, gave up the teaching as a hopeless task! Bernadette then persuaded her parents to take her back to Lourdes so that she could make her First Communion there. The little shepherdess left the sunny hills of Bartres in January of 1858 and returned home to the dark, damp room of the old jail. She attended the hospice, a school taught by the Sisters of Charity of Nevers.

On one cold day, Thursday, February 11, 1858, Bernadette, her sister, 'Toinette, and one of her neighbors, Jeanne Abadie, started off near noon to look for firewood along the banks of the Gave River, a stream which tumbles and rolls down the mountains and winds in and around Lourdes. The three girls cut across a meadow and passed alongside the Mill of Savy, which was operated by the waters of a channel from the main stream which wound around a huge cliff. In this cliff, called Massabielle, nature had hollowed out a sort of cave and grotto.

The girls decided to follow the channel to the spot where it joined the river. This brought them in front of the grotto. The mill was closed that day and the Gave River was low at the time, so the meeting place of the two streams was shallow. 'Toinette and Jeanne waded across. Bernadette looked around to see if she could cross without getting her feet wet. She didn't want to take off her shoes and stockings because of her asthma. She saw no possibility. She called to the girls to throw in some rocks so that she could cross. They told her to cross as they had done. Bernadette began to pull off her shoes and stockings.

Suddenly, Bernadette heard a sound like a gust of strong wind. Turning, she looked around but saw no movement in the leaves of the trees and shrubbery in the meadow. She began to pull off her second stocking but stopped short, for she heard the sound again, louder and clearer.

Looking up in the direction of the grotto, Bernadette was startled by the sight of a beautiful Lady in white standing there. She rubbed her eyes and looked again. The Lady was still there. Grabbing her rosary out of her pocket, she tried to make the Sign of the Cross but found that she could not lift her arm. She felt paralyzed with fear and amazement.

The Lady smiled sweetly, took her own beautiful rosary and made the Sign of the Cross. Bernadette, watching her, tried again to make the Sign of the Cross and succeeded. All fear disappeared. She fell to her knees and said the rosary in the presence of the beautiful Lady. When the rosary was finished, the Lady made a sign for Bernadette to come to her, but Bernadette was still too astonished to move. The beautiful Lady then slowly disappeared. Finally, Bernadette took off her stocking, waded across the stream and joined the other two girls.

On their way home, Bernadette asked the girls if they had seen anything at the grotto.

"No," they replied. "Why, did you?"

"Oh, I was just wondering," said Bernadette.

By her answer and because she had taken so long in joining them, they began to suspect that she had a secret. They pestered her until she finally revealed it on condition that they would not tell anyone.

'Toinette could not keep the secret. As soon as she reached home, she told her mother. Fearing that Bernadette was being deceived by some illusion, even perhaps by the devil, Mrs. Soubirous told Bernadette that she was not to go back to the grotto.

The more Bernadette thought about the beautiful Lady, the more convinced she was that she could not have been deceived by one so heavenly. That night while praying the rosary, Bernadette could not hold back the tears. It worried Mrs. Soubirous to see her daughter so upset, but she again told Bernadette that she was not to go back to the grotto.

By the following Sunday, such a strong power seemed to be drawing Bernadette to the grotto that she pleaded with her mother to allow her to go. Five or six little friends, anxious to see the grotto, pleaded with her also. Finally, her mother consented after they had promised to take holy water with them. The girls had just begun the rosary when the beautiful Lady appeared to Bernadette, who, mindful of her mother's orders, sprinkled holy water three times in the direction of the vision and told the Lady that if she were a messenger of God to come forward. The Lady smiled and advanced toward Bernadette. Bernadette finished the rosary with her companions and became so enrapt in the presence of the beautiful Lady that she was unaware of anything around her.

The following Thursday, two members of Our Lady's Sodality went with Bernadette to the grotto. They took with them some blessed candles, paper, pen and ink. As soon as they arrived, Bernadette saw the Lady waiting for her. Bernadette begged her to write down her wishes. The beautiful Lady told her that there was no need to write what she had to say. She desired Bernadette to return to the grotto every day for two weeks. Bernadette promised she would if her parents would consent. The Lady then told Bernadette that although she would not have the fleeting happiness of this world, she would possess eternal happiness in the next. Bernadette's joy was outwardly evident. She remained absorbed in prayer for about an hour. Then the Lady disappeared.

With her parents' permission, Bernadette kept her promise to visit the grotto daily, and the beautiful Lady rewarded those visits by appearing to Bernadette eighteen times.

As news of the apparitions spread, people from near and far began to flock to the grotto if only to get a

glimpse of Bernadette. This did not please the town officials, who tried to frighten Bernadette and her father and
to ridicule the whole affair. Their threats did not amount
to much. Bernadette had promised the beautiful Lady
that she would visit her daily, and she was determined
to keep her promise.

The beautiful Lady strengthened her little confidante
by revealing personal secrets to her. She begged for
prayers for poor sinners, pleaded for sacrifice and penance, and pointed out to Bernadette the miraculous spring
whose waters would cure many people in soul and body.

The existence of this spring had not been known.
The spring was still underground when the Lady told
Bernadette to drink and wash at it. Thinking the Lady
meant the Gave, Bernadette had turned in the direction
of the river. The Lady stopped her and pointed toward a
spot in the corner of the grotto. Bernadette dug the earth
with her hands, and the little hole she made filled up
with water immediately. After drinking some of it, she
washed her face as she had been told to do. The water
kept trickling through the hole. In a very short time it
made a channel for itself among the rocks. Ever-flowing
and crystal clear, Lourdes water has effected marvelous
cures for sufferers all over the world. It is used with
faith, love and devotion in honor of the beautiful Lady,
Mary, the Mother of God.

On her eleventh visit, the beautiful Lady told
Bernadette to tell the priest that she wanted a chapel
built at the grotto. Bernadette went straight to the rectory
and told the pastor, Father Peyramale, about the Lady's
request. The prudent priest had taken no part in the
happenings at the grotto. He felt that if the apparitions
were truly from heaven, divine Providence would make
this definitely known in time. So he was patiently waiting. He was amazed at Bernadette's detailed account of

the apparitions and at her simplicity. But he did not let her see his amazement. He simply told her that he was not in the habit of dealing with people he did not know, and therefore he insisted on knowing the Lady's name and on having evidence that she had a right to the requested chapel.

Three days later, on the fourteenth visit, the Lady told Bernadette to tell the priest she wanted processions made to the grotto. Poor Bernadette went slowly to the rectory. She feared her pastor more than she did the police. Since she did not know the Lady's name, she felt her reception would be a cold one.

When Father Peyramale heard about the processions, he excitedly told Bernadette that either she had made all this up or that the Lady was simply playing a role, for if it were from heaven she should have known that such a message should have been sent to the bishop and not to him. He added that if the Lady wanted a means to prove who she was, then he would suggest that she make the wild rose bush on which she was in the habit of standing, bloom suddenly in the presence of the crowd. Bernadette smiled at the suggestion as she left the rectory.

It was not necessary for such a miracle to take place. There was no need for it. There had already been many miracles: the miraculous spring, many cures and many conversions, the flocking crowds, Bernadette's transfiguration at prayer before the heavenly Lady.

On March twenty-fifth, the feast of the Annunciation, after Bernadette had pleaded with her three times, the beautiful Lady finally revealed: "I am the Immaculate Conception." Then she disappeared.

Bernadette hurried to the rectory. Now she had the treasured name of the beautiful Lady for her pastor. Bernadette did not understand the meaning of the words she had just heard, but she felt that Father would. Fearing to forget them, she repeated them over and over all the way to the rectory. When Father Peyramale heard them, he could not hide his emotions. Bernadette was surprised to see her stern old pastor so moved. Father dismissed her gently yet quickly.

To the priest and to the faithful no doubt now remained as to who had appeared at the grotto. It was Mary, the Queen of heaven, giving her approval to a dogma which had been proclaimed by the Holy See four years before. On December 8, 1854, Pope Pius IX had proclaimed the dogma of the Immaculate Conception, stating to the world the belief of the Church that Mary, from the first moment of her conception, was preserved free from the stain of original sin. Our Lady's appearance to Bernadette as the Immaculate Conception was a revelation to the world of the truth of the teachings of God's Church.

Bernadette saw our Lady at the grotto twice after that. Then, no more. On April seventh, absorbed in ecstasy before our Lady, Bernadette accidentally held her left hand over the flame of the candle in her right. The people around her gasped. Although the flames passed between her fingers for fifteen minutes, she felt no pain, and her hand showed no sign of burning. A doctor who saw this wished to experiment. After the ecstasy was over, he tried to see if Bernadette would react the same way, but she drew back quickly, saying that he was burning her.

On July sixteenth, the feast of Our Lady of Mount Carmel, our Lady again appeared to Bernadette, even though by this time, the police had barricaded the grotto. Since they could not gain entrance to the grotto, Bernadette and her aunt crossed the Gave River and knelt facing the Rock of the Apparition. Our Lady's smile and glance were directed to them across the barrier. Bernadette said that never was our Lady's smile so heavenly as in this last visit. Bernadette saw her no more on this earth.

The people, meanwhile, continued to flock to the grotto. The barricades were thrown down and pitched into the river. When they were put up again and a guard was placed there, the guard was entertained by one group of women while another group would switch places so that both had a chance to pray at the grotto. When this was discovered, a few arrests were made and court trials were held. When the complaints of the people reached the Emperor, Napoleon III, who happened to be in a town near Lourdes, he ordered the town officials to remove the barriers at the grotto and not to meddle any further there.

There were a number of reasons why the barriers had been erected. The town officials felt that they were responsible for order in the town. When the news of the apparitions began to spread, people from all over came flocking into Lourdes. Then, there were some free thinkers who denied the possibility of miracles and thought Bernadette was imagining things or else mentally affected, so they disapproved of the whole affair. Another reason was that since the Church had not yet declared anything concerning the apparitions, some, especially the prefect, felt that the public devotions at the grotto were superstitious and would bring harm to the Church.

The Church was bidding her time. In all patience she was waiting for fuller light. When Father Peyramale was convinced of Bernadette's sincerity, and when there was no further doubt in his mind concerning our Lady's apparitions, he went to Bishop Lawrence, who had also been patiently and attentively waiting. On July 28, 1858, a Commission of Investigation was formed. It was ordered to spare no means to arrive at the truth of the apparitions.

The Commission, composed of learned and holy priests, did not consider four years too much time to devote to proving the truth of something so gravely important. Eminent scientists and doctors worked with them, examining the water, the cures, the grotto, Bernadette. Nothing was overlooked. In 1862, Bishop Lawrence solemnly declared in the name of the Church that the faithful were justified in believing in all truth that our Lady had really appeared to Bernadette Soubirous eighteen times at the grotto in Lourdes.

Mindful of our Lady's request for a church and for processions, the Bishop gave his approval, and the work began at once. The first ceremony to take place at the scene of the apparitions was the blessing of the marble statue of our Lady, made by a holy sculptor according to Bernadette's description. Although it did not "measure up" to our Lady's beauty, when placed in the niche where our Lady appeared, the statue was beautiful. Bernadette liked it.

Desiring to leave the grotto untouched, Father Peyramale had the church built on top of the rock. There are really three churches, one built on the top of the other. The crypt or lower church was consecrated on May 21, 1866. Our Lady had prepared the way for the coming of her divine Son in that hallowed spot. The Mass was said by the Bishop himself, and Bernadette, in the midst of the Children of Mary, felt very close to her beautiful Lady and to Jesus present on the altar. In 1873, the first great National French Pilgrimage was inaugurated.

Later the magnificent basilica was also consecrated, and the statue of Our Lady of Lourdes was solemnly crowned. A special feast was established, and today it is observed by the entire Church on February eleventh— feast of Our Lady of Lourdes.

Bernadette remained for two years with her parents after the apparitions. They had moved from the old jail to a mill at the foot of the fort. Then she went to live as a boarder at the hospice, attending the school there. Once, while there, she became so very ill that she was near death's door. But at her request, she was given Lourdes' water to drink and she got well.

Shortly after the blessing of the marble statue at the grotto, Bernadette obtained permission to become a Sister of Charity and Christian Instruction of Nevers. Since the sisters knew her so well, her postulancy lasted only a few weeks. She received the habit and the name of Sister Marie Bernarde and began her novitiate at Nevers.

During November of that same year, 1866, she became very ill because of asthma, coughing and hemorrhage. The sisters feared she would die. She received Viaticum and the Anointing of the Sick and was allowed to pronounce her vows of poverty, chastity and obedience. This seemed to revive her, for she soon regained her strength and shortly afterward was up and around again. When she completed her novitiate training, she made her profession with the other novices, October 13, 1867.

Bernadette's mother, who had grieved much over her daughter's departure from home, died on the feast of the Immaculate Conception, December 8, 1866, while Bernadette was still a novice. The following year, with the aid of Father Peyramale, Bernadette's father, Francis Soubirous, was made proprietor of the Lacade Mill on the Lapaca Brook. The family then was in better circumstances.

In going about the ordinary duties of religious life, Sister Marie Bernarde edified her sisters greatly by her humility, her spirit of mortification, her charity and especially her spirit of self-abandonment to the holy will of God. As sacristan and as infirmarian her kindness was evident to all. The sick especially appreciated her goodness. When she became bedridden because of asthma, tuberculosis and caries of the bones, she united her sufferings to those of Christ. She had learned to smile at Mary. Now on her bed of pain she learned to smile at her cross.

One day the Mother Superior went to see Sister Marie Bernarde. She greeted her and asked what she was doing. In sweet simplicity Sister answered that she was doing her job. When asked what that job was, she answered, "I am being sick." Her spirit of resignation to the will of God was extraordinary. She suffered long and much. Finally, after a terrible agony, she died on Easter Wednesday, April 16, 1879, seated in an armchair.

She was thirty-five years old. Only the year before, on September 22, 1878, she had pronounced her perpetual vows. After her death, veneration to Bernadette spread. She was called the saint of humility, the saint of simplicity, the saint of common sense, and our Lady's little confidante. Miracles grew in number. Her body was found incorrupt.

On July 14, 1925, Pope Pius XI proclaimed Bernadette blessed, and on December 8, 1933, amid joyous celebrations in St. Peter's beautiful basilica, he proclaimed her a saint.

Bernadette, the simple French peasant girl, had been chosen by our Lady to make known to the world her approval of the pronouncement of the Immaculate Conception. As our Lady's little messenger to the world, not only did Bernadette proclaim heaven's approval of the dogma, not only did she request the building of a magnificent basilica and ask for pilgrimages and processions, but she fulfilled in her own holy life our Lady's request of her children—love, prayer, penance.

Today hundreds of thousands of people from all over the world annually make pilgrimages to the grotto of Our Lady of Lourdes. The flags of all the nations and the great collection of votive offerings, especially crutches, bespeak the gratitude of those who have been blessed by Mary, our Immaculate Mother.

More than ever do the pilgrims visit our Lady. They join in the midnight candle-light procession, saying the rosary and singing the famous "Ave, Ave, Ave Maria" hymn as the procession starts from the grotto. The pilgrims go up the ramp above the crypt, down toward the spacious boulevard, which is lined on both sides with beautiful trees in which hidden microphones clearly send out the voices of the leading choir. When they reach the beautiful life-size statue of the Sacred Heart, they turn back toward the basilica. The wave of candle light of the seemingly never-ending line of on-coming pilgrims and the swelling chorus of greetings to Mary fill the hearts of the pilgrims with increasing faith, hope and love. Arriving at the entrance of the basilica, the pilgrims join together, no matter their nationality, to recite the Nicene Creed in Latin. Then follows a private visit to the grotto, where all is quiet, except for the lapping waters of the Gave. No one speaks there above a necessary whisper. Peace, a heaven-sent peace, fills the soul, and one feels close to God and to Mary.

Miracles are still taking place at Lourdes, miracles of body and mostly miracles of soul. Every day at about 2:00 P.M. the sick are wheeled, rolled or helped in some way to the grotto. They are arranged in an orderly fashion, facing the grotto. Then begins the procession of the Blessed Sacrament. A bishop or priest passes along with the monstrance, blessing the sick. It is then that cures take place if heaven so chooses. A spirit of prayer, of penance, and of peace fills the atmosphere. It is wonderful to see the faith of the people, some kneeling saying the rosary, some with arms outstretched, and others devoutly kissing the black rock on which our Lady appeared. Others drink the water of the spring, which has been piped so that it flows freely from faucets beside the grotto, while others take baths in the healing waters. Others practice charity, aiding the sisters in their service to our Lady through her sick and her pilgrims. Still others prepare to make the Stations of the Cross on the mount by going up the stairway to the first station on their knees. Full of faith, love, penance and prayers, Mary's devotees receive their reward sooner or later from Our Lady of Lourdes, the Immaculate Conception.

The United States should have special devotion to the Immaculate Conception because the American hierarchy declared our Lady the national patroness of the United States under this title in 1846. By prayer and penance all should try to draw closer to Mary so that some day her "welcoming smile" will be seen as the angel of death ushers each one of us into the awe-inspiring presence of God.

III

Our Lady of Fatima

The flaming sun!
The glowing sun!
The dancing sun!
The spinning sun!
Who ever saw such a sight?
Ask the seers of Fatima
And the crowd in rainbow-light,
As they stood in the rain-soaked cova
On that memorable heaven-picked day,
Assembled to witness the miracle
And to hear what Mary would say.
Mary, Lady of the Rosary,
In solemn majesty,
Revealed to all, her requests of love
Through her humble, favored "three."
Lucy, Francis, Jacinta!
How well they knew her plea,
To say the Rosary devoutly
And to help set souls free
Through sacrifice and penance
And consecrated love,
To pray for those who pray not,
For the sake of heaven above.
Their lives have mirrored our Lady's
In a humble, simple way.
To you they hold out their treasures;
Make use of them every day:
The scapular, Mary's consecration badge,
With joy fills the heart,
The rosary, her Son's life-chaplet,
Causes her to do her part
In fulfilling her promise
Of intercession so true;
Her mother's heart yearns
For me and for you.

World War I began in 1914. Almost all of the European countries were affected by it. Portugal was one of these. In 1916, the guardian angel of Portugal prepared the way for our Lady's visits to Fatima, a small town sixty miles northeast of Lisbon.

Three children, Jacinta Marto, age six, Francis, her brother, age eight, and Lucy Santos, her cousin, age nine, were tending sheep in a large, hilly pasture which belonged to Lucy's father. When it started to rain, the children ran to take shelter in a cave in the hilly section. They still had a good view of the sheep. They ate their lunch and said the rosary as was customary among the country people for miles around. But they said their rosary in a very peculiar fashion. In order to save time for play, they said the first two words of the Our Father on the large beads and the first two words of the Hail Mary on the small beads, so they finished quickly. Of course, they were not saying the rosary properly, but they realized that only later on. Since it was still raining, the three children simply waited and watched the sheep.

After a while they noticed a bright, white light moving above the olive trees toward the cave. They stared speechless as the bright glow came nearer. In the center they saw a young man in a shining, flowing robe. When he was near, he smiled at them and said, "Fear not. I am the angel of peace. Pray with me." He knelt, touching his forehead to the ground. The children fell on their knees and repeated after him three times these words: "Oh, my God, I believe in you, I adore you, I hope in you, and I love You. I ask pardon for those who do not believe, do not adore, do not hope, and do not love you."

He arose, smiled down upon them again and told them to pray in such a way that Jesus and Mary would hear their prayers. Then he disappeared. The children were astonished and awestruck. They were not bound to secrecy about the vision, but they felt that it was so sacred that they did not speak of it to anyone.

Later in mid-summer, the angel came again. The three little shepherds had come home from the pasture for a few hours because of the intense heat. They were resting near a well in the grove behind Lucy's house. The angel stood before them. "Pray much," he said. "The hearts of Jesus and Mary have something for you to do. Offer up prayers and sacrifices to God." Lucy found her voice and asked how they were to make sacrifices. "Make everything you do a sacrifice and offer it as an act of reparation for the sins by which God is offended and as a petition for the conversion of sinners. Bring peace to our country in this way. I am the guardian angel of Portugal. Accept and bear with submission the suffering sent you by the Lord." Then he was gone, leaving the children deeply impressed.

In the autumn when the children were back in the same hilly pasture, the angel came for a third visit. He appeared to them holding a chalice in one hand and a host in the other hand. Drops of blood from the host fell into the chalice. Then leaving the chalice and the host suspended in the air, he prostrated himself on the ground and said the following prayer three times: "Most Holy Trinity, Father, Son, and Holy Spirit, I adore you profoundly, I offer you the most precious body, blood, soul and divinity of Jesus Christ present in all the tabernacles of the world, in reparation for the insults, sacrileges and indifference whereby he is offended. By the infinite merits of his most Sacred Heart and of the Immaculate Heart of Mary, I beg of you the conversions of sinners."

Rising, he took the chalice and the host. He gave the host to Lucy and the contents of the chalice to Jacinta and Francis, saying, "Receive the body and the blood of Jesus Christ. Make reparation for the crimes of sinners and give consolation to your God." Then he was gone.

Weeks and months passed and the little shepherds often thought of the angel of peace. They hoped and prayed that he would come back, but he never did. The two prayers which he taught them remained fresh in their memories. They said them often and tried to do as the angel had told them, to make sacrifices and to pray much.

About a year after the first visit of the angel, on May 13, 1917, something extraordinary happened. As was their daily custom, the three children were tending the sheep. This day it was in the Cova da Iria, about a mile from their homes. The field sloped as though someone had scooped out the center. There were a few olive and oak trees, but they were all small. It was a lovely sunshiny day.

The children ate their lunch at noon, said their fast rosary, and were ready for play. Since there were many loose stones in the field, they decided to build a stone house. As they ran across the field to gather the stones, a sudden flash of lightning surprised them.

Fearful of a storm even though the cloudless blue sky seemed to reassure them, the children decided to go home. As they headed for the center of the field and the sheep, another blinding flash frightened them. Startled, they looked around. They were attracted by a glowing light coming from the top of a small oak tree. The light was flowing from the form of a beautiful Lady whose feet were hidden in a shimmering white cloud resting on the tree. She was more beautiful than the angel. She wore a long white dress. At the neck was a long golden cord ending in a tassel. The white mantle that covered her head and fell to her feet was edged in gold. Her hands were joined in prayer. From her right hand hung a lovely rosary of white pearls with a brilliant white crucifix. She was brighter than the sun. The children were astonished and afraid. In a gentle voice the beautiful Lady told them not to fear, that she would not hurt them. Then Lucy asked who she was, where she came from, and what she wanted.

The Lady answered that she had come from heaven. She wanted them to come to the Cova on the thirteenth day of each month until October, then she would tell them who she was. Lucy asked if she was going to go to heaven. The Lady said that she would go, but that she must say the rosary and say it properly. When asked about Jacinta and Francis, the Lady agreed that Jacinta would go but that Francis would have to say many rosaries first. Lucy inquired about two girls who had died some time before. She was told that one was in heaven and the other in purgatory.

The Lady asked the children if they were willing to offer themselves to God, to bear all the sufferings he would send them, and to pray for sinners. Lucy answered that they were willing. The Lady added that they would have much to suffer, but God's grace would assist them. She opened her hands and from each palm a stream of light shone on the children.

She reminded them to say the rosary devoutly for world peace; then she turned toward the east and slowly disappeared.

At first Francis had not seen her. After saying a decade of his rosary, as the Lady had recommended, he saw her clearly. Only Lucy and Jacinta had heard her. Francis had heard nothing. Lucy told Francis all that the Lady had said.

When the angel had visited them the year before, after his visits they had felt physically tired with no desire to speak of what had happened. Our Lady's visit was different. It left the children jubilant, joyous, light. But Lucy felt it was wiser to say nothing to anyone about the Lady. When they parted that afternoon, they agreed to keep her visit a secret.

When Francis and Jacinta arrived home, they found out that their father and mother had gone to buy a pig. Francis busied himself about the yard, but Jacinta watched for her mother. It had been too much excitement for seven-year-old Jacinta, and she had never kept anything from her mother. As soon as her mother came in sight, Jacinta ran to tell her about the Lady. Her mother made light of it first, but, seeing the child's excitement and joy, she made her repeat everything to her father when he entered the house. Francis backed up her story.

The next morning, Jacinta's mother told her neighbors. Before long the whole of Fatima knew the story. Lucy's sister was the first in her family to hear the news. She questioned a surprised Lucy. When Lucy's mother heard the news, at first she merely laughed over such a possibility. When she found out that practically all of Fatima knew of the apparition, she began to realize the seriousness of the matter. She became very angry with Lucy, feeling that she was just trying to get attention and was not telling the truth. She scolded Lucy and punished her. The three children were then marched off to see their pastor to confess their "lies." The priest was kind and sympathetic. He would not pass judgment without further evidence.

The parents of Jacinta and Francis, especially their father, believed the children. The Martos were understanding, kind and patient. But Lucy's lot was a hard one. Her mother scolded and punished, and her brothers and sisters teased and made fun of her. Many of the neighbors ridiculed the children and their parents.

The annual celebration for the feast of St. Anthony was on June thirteenth. This was a big festival day in Fatima with music, dancing and refreshments. The children had always enjoyed the festivities, especially Jacinta, who loved to dance. As the day approached, the two mothers tried to encourage the children to forget the

Cova and to go to the feast. But the three children were determined to keep their promise to the Lady.

At the appointed time, at noon, the three children were kneeling before the small oak tree, which was about three feet high. Suddenly there was a flash of lightning, and our Lady stood over the tree. Lucy spoke to our Lady, who told her to insert between the mysteries of the rosary the aspiration "O my Jesus, forgive us our sins and save us from the fires of hell. Lead all souls to heaven, especially those in most need of your mercy." Our Lady told Lucy to learn to read and write. After speaking she said that Jacinta and Francis would go to heaven soon and that Lucy would some day spread devotion to the Immaculate Heart of Mary. Then Mary disappeared.

A few people had come to the Cova. They had seen a small cloud over the tree and had heard the sound of a very gentle voice speaking with Lucy, but they had not been able to understand what was said. It had been more like the gentle humming of a bee. Everyone wanted to know what Mary had said. The children answered that our Lady wanted the rosary said well, and that the rest was a secret. Then everyone wanted to know the secret. The children had no peace, but they were determined to keep secret what our Lady had said. Even the pastor began to doubt them and to say that perhaps this was a trick of the devil.

Another month of tortment went by for Lucy. Our Lady had told her that she would suffer a great deal. Through prayer and sacrifice the three children were able to strengthen themselves. Poor Lucy had the hardest struggle. She began to doubt and to fear. On the twelfth of July she told her cousins she would not go to the Cova the next day. They said they were going because the Lady had asked them to do so. Jacinta began to cry. Lucy said that if the Lady asked for her, to tell her she feared she was the devil.

The next morning Lucy still felt the same doubts, but, when it was time to leave for the Cova, all doubts disappeared. She rushed to find Jacinta and Francis, who were at home crying bitterly. They had been afraid to go without Lucy. The three then set out for the Cova. Many people had come from near and far, drawn by devotion or by curiosity.

When our Lady came, Lucy asked her to perform a miracle everyone could see so that they would believe. Our Lady promised a miracle in October and said that she would say who she was and what she desired then. Lucy had received many petitions from the people. Our Lady said that some would be answered and others would not be. Our Lady asked for sacrifices for sinners. She then opened her hands, and the light reflecting from them seemed to penetrate the earth as the children saw a sea of fire. In the fire were the devils and souls with human forms swaying and falling on every side amid wails and cries of pain and despair. Frightened, the three children raised their eyes to our Lady for help. She told them that they had seen hell where the souls of poor sinners go. God wanted to establish devotion to the Immaculate Heart to save sinners. Our Lady predicted another and worse war if people did not stop offending God. A night illumined by an unknown light would be the sign. If the world would heed her request, Russia would be converted; if not, Russia would spread errors throughout the world, causing persecutions and wars. In the end, Russia would be consecrated to her; it would be converted and some time of peace would be given the world. She told Lucy to tell all this to no one except to Francis. Then our Lady slowly disappeared.

The inquisitive crowd surrounded the children and almost smothered them. They wanted to know why the children looked so sad. Lucy said that it was a secret and she would not tell. Jacinta's father picked up Jacinta in his strong arms and they headed for home.

After this visit of the Lady, the children longed to be alone to say their prayers and to make sacrifices for sinners. News of the apparitions had spread throughout the country, and visitors began to come daily. They wanted to see the Cova and to speak with the children. The children had little peace.

The village of Fatima belonged to the County of Ourem whose chief magistrate was Arthur Santos, a man of tremendous political power. A baptized Catholic, he had given up his Faith. He published the local newspaper and tried in every possible way to undermine the people's faith in the Church and in the priests.

Santos heard about the apparitions of Fatima and feared the effects on the people. He was determined to crush all this to prevent renewed life in the Church.

He summoned Lucy, her father and Jacinta's father to the county house at twelve noon on August eleventh. He tried to get the secret from Lucy. She refused to tell him. He questioned the two fathers, but got very little from them. He dismissed them, but told Lucy that if he did not learn her secret he would take her life. They returned home thinking they were through with him. But Santos was determined that the children would not be at the Cova for the next apparition.

On the morning of August thirteenth, pretending that he was interested in our Lady, Santos managed to get the children to his carriage, saying he would ride them to the Cova. Instead, he took them to his home in Ourem. He locked them in a room, warning them that they would not get out until they told him the secret. The magistrate's wife was kind to them. She gave them a good lunch and allowed them to play on the veranda with her children.

Meanwhile at the Cova, thousands of people had gathered. They prayed and sang hymns around the small oak tree. When they found out that the children had been kidnapped and could not come, a terrible resentment went through the crowd. Just then a clap of thunder resounded, and a flash of lightning was seen.

A little white cloud came and stopped right over the oak. It stayed a few minutes, then rose toward the heavens and disappeared. As it did so, the people looked around at one another. Their faces and clothes glowed in all the colors of the rainbow. Everything was transformed in a rainbow of colors: the trees, the grass, the rocks. Then all slowly went back to normal. Everyone realized that our Lady had come, but not finding the children, she had returned to heaven.

Furious and angry, the crowd was ready to go to Ourem to protect the children. Jacinta's father calmed them and told them that those who needed punishment would get it, and that God was allowing all to happen for a purpose. The crowd then dispersed quietly, with the realization that our Lady had really come.

The children spent a lonely night fearful of what might happen. The next morning they were taken to the county house where they were questioned, offered all kinds of promises, and then threatened, but they would not tell the secret. That afternoon they had to go through the same ordeal as in the morning. Finally, the furious magistrate said that they had to go to jail and that he would throw them into a tank of boiling oil unless they told him their secret. When they were brought to jail, Jacinta began to cry, not because she feared the jail but because she thought she would have to die without seeing her parents.

The many prisoners were touched by the three children. They tried to console them and to encourage them to tell the secret. But they said that they would rather die than reveal it. To distract them, the men began to sing and to dance. When the children knelt to say the rosary, the men knelt also and joined in prayer with them. Shortly after that, they were taken back to the county house.

Jacinta was called in first and told that the oil was boiling and that she had better tell her secret, but she remained silent. She was ordered to be thrown in. A guard took a fearful Jacinta and locked her in another room. Francis was next. He was told to tell the secret. He refused. He was ordered to share his sister's lot. He was locked up in the same room with a relieved Jacinta.

Lucy was sure that they had been killed. Fearful, yet trusting in our Lady, she awaited her turn. She told the magistrate what she had told her parents and the pastor, but she would not tell the secret; so she too was locked up with Jacinta and Francis. The magistrate, seeing that he was accomplishing nothing, brought them back to Fatima in his carriage. What he had done had only helped to publicize the events at the Cova all the more.

On August nineteenth, our Lady appeared to the children in another pasture as a reward for being faithful. She told them to continue to go to the Cova on the thirteenth and to say the rosary every day. She also said that the miracle on October thirteenth would not be as great because of the affair in Ourem. She encouraged them to pray much and to sacrifice much for sinners. Then she disappeared. After this visit the children redoubled their zeal for sacrifices and prayer.

On September thirteenth, there were about 30,000 people present in the Cova. The crowd was so great that the children had a hard time making their way to the oak tree. At noon, the people saw a globe of light descend from the east and settle on the tree. It was followed by the bright white cloud. Then from the clear sky white petals, like manna, began to fall, but they dissolved before they came within reach.

Our Lady spoke to the children, encouraging them in their prayers and sacrifices. She again stated that in October she would perform a miracle so that all would believe.

Lucy repeated our Lady's promise of a miracle on October thirteenth. The news spread like a wildfire throughout the country. People came from near and far to be present for the miracle. It is believed that about 70,000 persons crowded into the Cova even though it was raining. Lucy's mother was worried for her daughter. She feared what might happen to Lucy if there were no miracle. Lucy tried to calm her mother's fears. She knew that there would be a miracle; our Lady had promised.

The apparition began as it always had: first the thunder, the flash of lightning, then the cloud. Our Lady stood over the oak. She told the children that she was the Lady of the Rosary and that she wanted a chapel built in the Cova in her honor. They must continue to say the rosary devoutly every day. The war would soon end, and the soldiers would return home. When favors were requested, our Lady said that some would be granted but others would not be. People must change their ways and not keep offending our Lord, who is so greatly offended.

As our Lady took leave of the children, she opened her hands. Beams of light shone forth. While she was rising, she pointed to the sun which had been hidden by clouds. The rain had now stopped. To the left of the sun, the three children saw St. Joseph, who held the Child

Jesus in his arms. He blessed the world three times. To the right of the sun, they saw our Lady dressed in the blue and white robes of Our Lady of the Rosary. Then Lucy alone saw our Lord, dressed in red as the Divine Redeemer, blessing the world. Beside Him stood Our Lady of Sorrows but without the sword. Lastly, she saw our Lady in the simple brown robes of Our Lady of Mount Carmel.

While the children were gazing at these representations, the crowd was witnessing a strange sight. The sun became very pale and changed to a silver disc. It threw shafts of light, casting different colors: blue, yellow, green, red, purple, orange, on everything around. The people could look at the sun with perfect ease. Then the sun stopped its play of light and began to dance and to spin. It stopped a while and then began to dance and spin again. Finally, it seemed to loosen itself from the sky and in a mighty zigzag motion hurled itself toward the earth. The people cried out in terror. Then the sun stopped short in its fall and zigzagged back to its normal position in the sky. A few minutes before that, the people had been standing in the rain, soaked to the skin. Now their clothes were perfectly dry.

After the last apparition, the three children tried to return to their ordinary routine life. But it was impossible. People flocked to see and to speak with them. Francis and Jacinta prayerfully waited for the day when Mary would take them to heaven.

In October 1918, the whole Marto family, with the exception of the father, became ill with influenza. Mr. Marto took care of the house, cooked meals, and nursed his large family. Francis' condition was the most serious. our Lady appeared to him and Jacinta to tell them she would take Francis to heaven soon, and that Jacinta would follow shortly afterward.

The attitudes of the two children were edifying. On April 14, 1919, our Lady came for Francis. Jacinta was too ill to attend her brother's funeral. Her condition grew worse, and an abscess formed on her chest. The doctor advised her parents to take her to the hospital at Ourem for treatments. She stayed there two months, undergoing much suffering, which she offered for the conversion of sinners. She was finally discharged since nothing could be done to help her. Later, a doctor who was interested in Jacinta had her taken to Lisbon in the hope that something could be done for her there. Jacinta's sufferings only increased. She died away from home on February 20, 1920. No member of the family was with her.

Lucy felt lonely now that her two little cousins were in heaven, but she knew our Lady would watch over her.

Thousands of visitors flocked to Fatima. They wanted to see Lucy and talk to her. Finally, in 1921, the bishop made plans to send Lucy to a convent boarding school where she would be unknown and no one would bother her. She was given another name, Maria das Dores, and was told not to speak of Fatima. The girls at school quickly learned to love her. She inspired a deep love for Mary in all. When she finished her course of studies, she asked to be admitted into the religious order that ran the boarding school, the Sisters of St. Dorothy.

Our Lady appeared to Lucy in the convent in December, 1925, and told her to practice and to promote devotion to her Immaculate Heart by means of the First Saturday devotions.

Our Lady promised to assist at the hour of death with graces necessary for salvation all those who, on the first Saturday of five consecutive months, go to confession and receive Holy Communion, recite the rosary and keep her company for a quarter of an hour while meditating on the mysteries of the rosary with the intention of making reparation to her.

On the night of January 24, 1938, Lucy saw extraordinary lights in the sky. That was the sign that God's justice was ready to strike the world. In March, 1938, Germany invaded Austria and prepared for World War II, which broke out in September, 1939.

In 1942 the Holy Father consecrated the whole world, with special mention of Russia, to the Immaculate Heart. Ten years later, in 1952, he specifically consecrated the people of Russia to the Immaculate Heart of Mary.

The secret of Fatima has been a puzzle to many. There are three parts to the secret. In 1941, with our Lady's permission, Lucy revealed the first two parts in a document sent to her bishop. The first was concerning the vision of hell and the second was about World War II and Communism in Russia. The third part has never been made public.

In response to our Lady's request, a small chapel was built at the Cova and a beautiful statue was placed within it. But in 1922 it was destroyed by atheists. Two bombs were placed in the Cova, one in the chapel and the other at the base of the oak tree. The roof of the chapel was blown off, but the bomb at the oak failed to explode. A new chapel was built on the site of the oak tree to replace one torn to pieces by souvenir hunters. A great pilgrimage of reparation was held on May 13, 1923. Over 60,000 persons gathered to pay homage to our Lady.

The bishop bought a large area of land surrounding the Cova and allowed Mass to be said there as early as 1921. Today the little chapel can still be seen, but the basilica of the Immaculate Heart of Mary, with altars in honor of each of the fifteen mysteries of the rosary, dominates the area. There are new and beautiful buildings all around: a hospital, monasteries, retreat houses, and others.

Lucy became a Carmelite nun in Coimbra, Portugal. Her life of prayer, reparation and consecration "preached" the message of Fatima.

Just as the rosary is the prayer primarily advocated at Fatima, so is the scapular of Our Lady of Mount Carmel the sign of consecration to the Immaculate Heart. Through the rosary and the scapular, Mary is given homage, confidence and love.

IV

Our Lady
of Good Counsel

Dear Lady, Jesus is your little boy.
He knows all, he can do all
For he is God.

As he whispers to you words of love
    and affection,
Plead for us counsel and protection.
You are his Mother, to whom he will listen.
We are your children, with life's tears aglisten.
O Mother, O Queen,
Lead us to the eternal light,
Protect us, counsel us to do the right,
So some day soon
We may share with you and your boy
Heaven's blessings and eternal joy.

Dear Lady, Jesus is your little boy.
He knows all, he can do all
For he is God.

There is a small town in Italy called Genazzano. It is about thirty miles southeast of Rome. Long before the coming of Christ, the people of the town had built a temple to the pagan goddess of love, Venus. Here they gave her special worship, and here they enjoyed fiestas and celebrations in her honor. One big day of celebration was April twenty-fifth. Every year the people of Genazzano spent the whole a day in joyous festivities. They danced, sang and feasted.

When Christianity was accepted, loved and outwardly practiced in the Roman Empire, this little town was likewise affected. In the fourth century, Pope St. Mark had a Catholic church built on the hill above the town, not too far from the ruins of the ancient pagan temple. The church was dedicated to Our Lady of Good Counsel. It was sturdy and strong, but small and plain. Knowing the love the people of Genazzano had for fiestas and celebrations, the Pope declared April twenty-fifth, until then a pagan feast, the Christian feast of Our Lady of Good Counsel.

Through the centuries, our Lady was honored in a special way in the little church on the hill. The friars of the Order of St. Augustine were given charge of the church in 1356.

Time, wear and tear began to affect the ancient building. By the fifteenth century the church had become so dilapidated that some feared it would fall apart. Few seemed to take an interest in it however, possibly because there were other newer and better churches in the town.

A holy widow, Petruccia de Geneo, who loved our Lady devoutly, felt inspired to rebuild the church. She wanted the new church to be larger and more beautiful, more befitting the Mother of God. Trusting in our Lady,

Petruccia hired workers and builders, purchased the needed materials and watched the walls go up. Her neighbors silently looked on for a while. Then they began to make fun of Petruccia, especially when she asked them for help.

Petruccia could not understand the attitude that her neighbors had taken. She felt that their own love for Mary should have prompted them to offer help. Some of the neighbors did not truly know Petruccia. They knew that to build a big and beautiful church was a great undertaking. They knew that Petruccia had money, but not that much. They felt that pride and presumption had made her dare such a thing as the building of a church. Instead of receiving the cooperation and support that she counted on, Petruccia was criticized. When the work had to stop because of lack of funds, the unfinished walls were labeled "Petruccia's Folly."

Probably our Lord permitted all this to strengthen Petruccia's love and trust. Jealousy, lack of charity, and misunderstanding sometimes step in to prevent one's sharing in a great work. But Petruccia was a holy soul. She was not going to let herself become downcast. She was determined to do all that she could to see the church completed. She felt that our Lady had inspired the work and that our Lady would support it when the time was ripe. She said that some day "a great Lady would come to take possession of it." Petruccia then had recourse to more fervent prayers and sacrifices.

Soon after, on a fiesta day for the town, St. Mark's Day, 1467, many people were gathered in the market square having a good time—feasting, dancing and singing. It is not known why they no longer honored Our Lady of Good Counsel on that day, April twenty-fifth, as their forebears had done in previous centuries. Perhaps through the centuries their devotion to our Lady had somewhat diminished, but they had retained their love for fiestas and fun. This fiesta coincided with the feast of St. Mark, which is celebrated by the universal Church on April twenty-fifth.

In the midst of the festivities, someone spied a fleecy cloud floating very low across the clear blue sky. The dancing and the singing stopped. All attention was focused on the slowly descending cloud which finally settled itself on the narrow ledge of the unfinished walls of Petruccia's church. The cloud gradually divided itself, and there in the midst was a beautiful picture of our Lady and the Child Jesus. All the church bells of the town began ringing loudly and clearly, without the help of human hands.

Attracted by the unexpected loud ringing of the resounding bells, people from the nearby villages rushed into Genazzano to find out the cause. Hearing of the miracle, Petruccia, who had been praying at home, hurried to the church to kneel before the picture. She joyfully said that she had known our Lady would come to take possession of *her* church. The people all joined her in praising our Lady.

No one knew where the picture had come from. No one had ever seen it before. Soon marvelous showers of graces and miraculous cures began to take place. Within four months 171 miracles were recorded. People began to call the picture the "Madonna of Paradise" because they believed it had been brought to Genazzano by the hands of angels, hidden in the fleecy cloud. Others, because of the numerous miracles, called it the "Miraculous Madonna."

In the meantime, two strangers, who had heard about the miraculous picture, came to Genazzano to see it. At sight of it, the two strangers, one an Albanian, the other, a Slav, agreed that they had seen the very picture a few weeks before in a church just outside of Scutari in Albania. They explained that they were refugees who had fled from Albania because the Ottoman Turks had captured it. Within a week the two men with their families and many Albanian friends, moved into Genazzano to live near their Madonna, who had also taken refuge from the Turks.

When the Holy Father in Rome heard about the miraculous picture and the many miracles, he sent two bishops as commissioners to examine and study the extraordinary happenings. After careful investigations, the Pope and the commissioners were convinced that the picture was really that of Our Lady of Good Counsel, which had been venerated for centuries in the little town of Scutari. The empty space with the exact dimensions where the picture had been in the church was evident to everyone. The picture—the thickness of an eggshell—had been painted on the wall plaster. No human skill could have successfully cut the thin wafer-like picture from the wall without cracking it. No human hands could have carried it across the Adriatic Sea and placed it on the narrow ledge with no back support whatever.

Naturally, Petruccia's church was completed. In fact, so many donations poured in and so much help was offered that it turned out to be a beautiful basilica. The picture was enshrined in a marvelous gold frame adorned with precious stones. Later, golden crowns sent by the Vatican were placed on the heads of the Madonna and the Child. The picture still stands secure on its base, "Petruccia's Folly." The Friars of St. Augustine are the special guardians of the church and of the miraculous picture.

The basilica has been affected by the centuries. Wars have touched it, especially World War II. In order to check the advance of the Allies, the Germans did not hesitate to bomb churches. At Genazzano, our Lady's shrine was not spared. A bomb exploded with full force in the sanctuary. The main altar was completely destroyed. The plaster paintings and the statues on surrounding walls came tumbling down. But the miraculous picture of Our Lady of Good Counsel, a few yards from the sanctuary, remained perfectly intact, as lovely as when Petruccia first saw it.

Our Lady has her eyes partly downcast as though she is intently listening. Her dark green dress is trimmed with a gold collar. Her bright blue mantle covers her head and shoulders and partly covers the Child Jesus, who has one arm around his Mother's neck. His cheek is touching hers, and his left hand is holding the collar of her dress. The Infant's red dress is trimmed with gold. The expressions of both Mother and Child are of rapt attention. The Child Jesus looks as though he is ready to whisper something to his Mother. It is a simple but appealing picture.

In the past four centuries many miracles have taken place at our Lady's shrine. Countless pilgrimages have been made to it. Our Lady has always proved herself a loving Mother and a treasurer of divine grace.

Go to her with your little problems; go to her with your big problems; trust in her guidance. She is truly our Mother of Good Counsel.

These words—"Mother of Good Counsel"—were inserted by Pope Pius IX into the litany of the Blessed Virgin.

V

Our Lady
of Perpetual Help

The joys and sorrows of the day
Are echoes of God's love;
The joys and sorrows of the day
Help shape our crown above.
Day by day, year by year,
We toil, we love, we pray,
We sing, we hope, we suffer, too,
Along our heavenward way.
When we view our crosses,
And troubles not so few,
Our Lady of Perpetual Help,
We do have need of you.
In union with our Savior,
Calvary's sorrows may we bear;
With our hands in yours, O Lady,
Redemptive love we ask to share;
Nature can't help but shudder
At the thought of cross and pain;
But the price of souls is costly,
Precious blood from God's own vein.
May the sacrificial spirit
That inspired your loving Son
Be ours, too, O Lady,
And heaven, for souls, be won.

In the fifteenth century a wealthy merchant lived on the island of Crete in the Mediterranean Sea. He had in his possession a beautiful painting of Our Lady of Perpetual Help.

How he got the picture is not known. Had he stolen it from the shrine where it had been publicly venerated for centuries? Had he been entrusted with it for safe-keeping because the enemies of Christianity had been conquering eastern Europe? History does not say. In any case, the merchant was determined that this picture would not be destroyed as so many others had been.

Painted on wood, the picture measures twenty-one by seventeen inches and is said to be a copy of the famous original painted by St. Luke. St. Luke's picture had been taken to Constantinople and had been vener-ated as miraculous for centuries. It was destroyed in 1453 when Constantinople was captured by the Turks. The faithful in Crete did not want this to happen to their picture of Mary.

The merchant decided to take the picture to Italy. He packed his belongings, settled his business, and boarded a vessel sailing for Rome. After the vessel was well on its way, a violent storm arose. The sailors and all on board feared the worst. The merchant quickly got out his picture of our Lady, held it aloft and called on her for help. Our Lady answered his prayer with a miracle. The sea grew calm, and the vessel reached the port of Rome safely.

The merchant had a dear friend living in Rome. He decided to spend some time with his friend before mov-ing on. He joyfully displayed our Lady's picture and told his friend that some day the whole world would pay honor to Our Lady of Perpetual Help.

Some time later, the merchant became very ill. When he felt that his days were numbered, he called his friend to his bedside and begged him to promise that after his death he would place our Lady's picture in a suitable church so that it could be venerated publicly. The friend promised.

Although he had meant to carry out the merchant's dying wish, the man neglected to do so. His wife had taken a great liking to the picture and persuaded him to keep it safe under their roof. But Divine Providence had not brought the picture to Rome for the veneration of one family, but for the veneration of the world, as the merchant had prophesied.

Our Lady appeared to the man on three different occasions, telling him that he must put her picture in a church. Then the man became gravely ill and died.

The man's wife was very attached to the picture and tried to convince herself that it was safest under her own roof. So she put off parting with it. One day, her six-year-old daughter came rushing to her with the news that a beautiful, shining Lady had appeared to her while she was looking at the picture. The Lady had told her to tell her mother and grandfather that Our Lady of Perpetual Help wanted to be placed in a church.

As the widow was wondering what church should be given the painting, heaven sent the answer. Our Lady appeared to the little girl again and told her to tell her mother that she wanted the picture placed in the church between the Basilica of St. Mary Major and that of St. John Lateran. That church was the Church of St. Matthew, the Apostle.

The lady went quickly to see the superior of the Augustinians, who had been entrusted with the care of St. Matthew's. She informed him of the circumstances connected with the picture. On March 27, 1499, the picture was carried to the church in solemn procession. On the way from the widow's house to the church, a man touched the picture and regained the use of his paralyzed arm.

The picture was hung over the high altar in the church. For about three hundred years it remained there. Loved and venerated by all in Rome as a truly miraculous picture, it was a means of countless miracles, cures and needed graces.

In 1798, Napoleon and his army captured Rome. He exiled Pope Pius VII and, under pretext of strengthening the defenses of Rome, destroyed thirty churches. St. Matthew's Church was one of these. Napoleon ordered it to be leveled to the ground. The church and many venerable relics and statues were completely destroyed to the utter dismay and grief of the Romans. The picture of Our Lady of Perpetual Help disappeared.

One of the Augustinian priests had secretly taken the picture away just in time.

When Pius VII finally returned to Rome, he gave the Augustinians the monastery of St. Eusebius and later the house and church of St. Mary's in Posterula.

A famous picture of Our Lady of Grace was already enshrined in St. Mary's in Posterula. So the miraculous picture of Our Lady of Perpetual Help was placed in the Augustinians' private chapel. For sixty-four years it remained there in the chapel almost forgotten.

In the meantime, at the request of the Pope, the superior general of the Redemptorists set up his headquarters in Rome. Land was purchased and a monastery and the church of St. Alphonsus were built. One of the priests, the historian of the house, made a special study of the section in Rome where they were living. In his research, he came across many references to the old Church of St. Matthew and the miraculous picture of Our Lady of Perpetual Help. One day he gave the other priests the information he had discovered: that their present church, St. Alphonsus, was built on the ruins of St. Matthew's, where a miraculous picture of Our Lady of Perpetual Help had been publicly venerated for centuries.

Among his hearers was Father Michael Marchi, who had served Mass many times as a boy in the chapel of the Augustinians in Posterula. There in the chapel he had seen the miraculous picture. An old lay brother, who had lived at St. Matthew's and whom he had often visited, had told him many times of the miracles worked by our Lady, and he would always add: "Mind, Michael, our Blessed Lady of St. Matthew's is the same picture that is in the private chapel. Don't forget it." Father Michael related all that he had learned from the old lay brother.

Through this incident, the Redemptorists had come to know of the existence of the picture, but they did not know its history, nor did they know that our Lady wished it to be publicly honored in a special place.

That very year, through an inspirational sermon preached by a Jesuit about the ancient picture of Our Lady of Perpetual Help, they learned the history of the picture and that our Lady wished it to be venerated between the Church of St. Mary Major and that of St. John Lateran. The holy Jesuit deplored the fact that for the last sixty years the picture, which had been so famous for miracles and cures, had disappeared and that there was no accounts of cures being worked in the area. He felt that this was because the picture was no longer exposed to the public veneration of the faithful. He pleaded with his hearers, asking that if anyone knew where the picture was they would acquaint the possessor with our Lady's wish.

The Redemptorist fathers longed to see the miraculous picture restored to public veneration and in their own Church of St. Alphonsus, if possible. They entreated their superior general to try to obtain the picture for St. Alphonsus' Church. After some deliberation and time, the superior decided to ask the intervention of the Holy

Father, Pope Pius IX. He related the history of the painting and submitted his petition.

The Holy Father listened attentively. He loved our Lady dearly and was happy to see her honored. He took his pen and wrote out his wish that the miraculous picture of Our Lady of Perpetual Help be returned to the church between St. Mary Major and St. John Lateran. He also commissioned the Redemptorists to make Our Lady of Perpetual Help known everywhere.

None of the Augustinians living at that time had known St. Matthew's. Some had forgotten the history of the picture in their chapel; others had never known it. Once they knew the history and the Holy Father's wish, they willingly complied with our Lady's desire. They had been her custodians, and now they were giving her back to the world under the care of other custodians. Divine Providence had set the stage. At the request of the Holy Father, the Redemptorists gave the Augustinians another painting to replace the miraculous one.

The picture of Our Lady of Perpetual Help was carried in solemn procession through the beautifully decked streets of Rome before being placed over an altar especially built for its veneration. The happiness of the Roman people was evident. The enthusiasm and joyous manifestations of the twenty thousand who thronged the flower-strewn streets for the procession proved their deep devotion to God's Mother. Every hour of the day, people of all classes could be seen before the picture, begging Our Lady of Perpetual Help to hear their prayers and to obtain mercy for them. Many miracles and graces were recorded daily.

Today, devotion to Our Lady of Perpetual Help has spread throughout the world. Churches have been dedicated in her honor, shrines have been built, and archconfraternities have been established. Her picture is known and loved near and far.

VI

Our Lady
of Mount Carmel

Heaven smiled down on man,
And the Queen, in response to a plea,
Brought a "grace-garment" to the earth,
To the man on bended knee.
The aged Simon embraced it
And spread its devotion abroad;
'Twas a life of consecration to Mary—
Mary, the Mother of the Lord.
To those who wear her garment
And pledge service to her Son,
She promises salvation—
Heaven eternally won.
Her children of predilection,
She chooses to set them free
From purgatorial fires on Saturday,
Provided they will to be.
O Queen of the Brown Cloth Scapular,
O beautiful "Star of the Sea,"
Guide all your Carmelite children
Who place loving trust in thee.

Mount Carmel is a beautiful mountain range in Palestine overlooking the Mediterranean Sea. It is not too far from Nazareth.

Around 850 B.C. the prophet Elijah lived a holy and penitential life on the heights of Mount Carmel. He saw a little cloud that rose over the sea, bringing rain and new life to the parched earth. This cloud prefigured our Lady.

Centuries later, when the Crusaders went to Palestine to rescue the Holy Land from the Mohammedans who had captured it, they were surprised to find a number of holy men living in caves on Mount Carmel. These holy men called themselves Hermits of Our Lady of Mount Carmel.

The Crusaders were very impressed by the hermits, who claimed to be successors of St. Elijah. The hermits had erected on Mount Carmel what they considered to be the very first chapel on earth dedicated to the Mother of God.

In 1145, St. Berthold organized the hermits into a community and began the construction of a monastery. In 1200, after St. Berthold's death, St. Brocard was elected father general. He completed the monastery on Mount Carmel and in 1210 obtained from St. Albert of Jerusalem a rule for the hermits to live by. This rule was approved by Pope Honorius III in 1226.

When the Crusaders returned to Europe, they brought back with them some of those holy men, who settled in England and in France. Simon Stock, a devout and holy man living in England, was so impressed with their dedication that he joined the hermits. He was sent to Mount Carmel, where he imbibed the true Carmelite spirit.

As the years went by, the persecutions by the Mohammedans increased and it became dangerous for the

Carmelites to remain in Palestine. In 1237, a special meeting or chapter was held on Mount Carmel. It was decided that for the good of the Order, the Carmelites would migrate to Europe. A few courageous hermits volunteered to stay in their beloved monastery on Mount Carmel. In 1291, the Mohammedans killed all the hermits and completely destroyed the monastery.

In 1241, Richard Grey, the Earl of Kent, gave the Carmelites a home on his vast estate at Aylesford, England, on the River Medway. The Carmelites at once began to build their hermitage which can still be seen today. The Bishop of Rochester encouraged them to build a church, which was dedicated to the Assumption of our Lady. New foundations were made elsewhere in England, but Aylesford was the main Carmelite center.

At the chapter meeting held in Aylesford in 1245, Simon Stock was elected first general of the Carmelite Order in the West. His brother hermits had become aware of his sanctity and qualities of leadership. The Order was going through troubled times and needed a saint at its head.

In order to aid the Church, the Carmelites had to change from hermits to friars. The active apostolate made its demands on them, and they had to adapt themselves to new conditions. They were, thenceforth, called the Brothers of Our Lady of Mount Carmel. The young Carmelites were sent to the universities, and Carmelite houses were established in university cities. This alarmed the older Carmelites, who had lived lives of solitude on Mount Carmel. They found the new ways both difficult and contradictory.

The secular clergy resented the presence of a strange new religious order in their midst. Not only did they persecute the Carmelites, but they carried their cries to Rome, demanding the newcomers to disband. The striped or barred cloak which the Carmelites wore was also very unpopular. Simon had thought of changing it because it was hindering the growth of the Order, but in deference to the older members who loved the ancient cloak, he did not.

For the first five years of his generalship, the dissatisfaction and opposition from within and from without grew stronger and stronger day by day. This was a heavy trial for Simon, who felt the weight of his years and the weight of his cross.

At that time, 1251, Simon Stock was eighty-six years old. He redoubled his prayers and pleadings to Our Lady of Mount Carmel. On the night of July fifteenth he sought the solitude of his cell and spent the entire night on his knees, beseeching our Lady to save her Order. His beautiful prayer, "Flos Carmeli," has come down to us: "Flower of Carmel, blossoming vine, splendor of heaven, Mother divine, none like to you! Mother of meekness, peerless you are! To the Carmelites favors impart, Star of the Sea!"

During the early morning of July 16, 1251, Simon's cell was flooded with a great light. Our Lady of Mount Carmel, accompanied by a multitude of angels, appeared to Simon, holding the scapular of the Order in her hands. She said to him: "Receive, my beloved son, this scapular of your Order. This shall be to you and to all Carmelites a privilege that whosoever dies clothed in this shall never suffer eternal fire. It is the badge of salvation, a protection in danger, a pledge of peace and eternal alliance."

Full of consolation and courage, and inspired by our Lady, Simon sent two of the Carmelites to the Pope. The Holy Father adopted the cause of the Carmelites and eventually took the Order, and all belonging to it, under the protection of the Holy See.

Simon wrote a detailed account of our Lady's visit and promise and sent it to all the Carmelite monasteries. Devotion to the scapular began to spread. Miracles began to take place by means of the scapular. When lay people learned of our Lady's promise, they, too, wanted the scapular and its benefits. Popes and bishops, kings and queens, nobles and peasants, all wanted to be invested in the brown scapular to obtain what our Lady had promised. A confraternity was formed to foster devotion to the scapular. Directly and indirectly, nineteen successive popes have blessed and approved the scapular devotion.

About twenty years after Simon Stock's death, a chapter was held in which the Carmelites decided to use a white cloak opening in the front so that the scapular, which was then considered the main part of the habit, could be seen. Up to that time the Carmelite cloak had been a circular, barred garment with a hole in the center for the head to go through. The scapular had been more of an apron to protect the tunic.

Our Lady made the scapular her special livery, a garment of salvation. The Germans call it the "grace-garment," and it *is* that if wisely used.

The Carmelites prospered in their work. They spread throughout western Europe, preaching the Faith wherever they went, building monasteries, teaching in universities and schools, leading a life of contemplative prayer and zealous work for souls. Noble and gifted men were attracted to the Order and it grew in numbers.

Meanwhile, the devil continued to stir up opposition. Envy played its part. Undaunted, the Carmelites continued to work for their Queen and Mother, Our Lady of Mount Carmel. And our Lady continued to work for her beloved sons and brothers.

In 1322, Our Lady of Mount Carmel appeared to Pope John XXII in Avignon, France, and urged him to take the Order of Mount Carmel under his special protection. She promised him that she would assist the souls of the members in purgatory and deliver them from their sufferings on the first Saturday after death if they fulfilled certain conditions. Pope John XXII issued a bull in which he stated all that our Lady had told him.

The conditions outlined by our Lady for gaining the Sabbatine Privilege were the observance of chastity according to one's state in life, the wearing of the scapular with devotion, and the daily recitation of the Little Office of the Blessed Virgin. If the recitation of the Office is impossible or gravely inconvenient, a priest with the proper faculties can permit a substitute. This could be abstinence from meat on Wednesday and Saturday, or the daily recitation of the rosary, or some other good work.

The Palace of the popes at Avignon is still in existence. It is one of the tourists' highlights. Adjoining it is a beautiful church in which a large painting depicts our Lady's appearance to Pope John XXII. The bull concerning the Sabbatine Privilege was issued to the Carmelites on March 3, 1322. In 1409, Pope Alexander V approved and confirmed it in Rome. Other succeeding popes did likewise. When rash critics attacked the apparition, Pope Benedict XIV openly and heroically defended it. Satan was not going to let such a privilege for the salvation of souls spread without a struggle.

The feast of Our Lady of Mount Carmel was instituted for the Carmelites in 1332. It was later extended to the universal Church by Pope Benedict XIII in 1726.

In the fourteenth century a terrible plague called the "Black Death" swept over Europe. Thousands of people died. The Carmelites heroically did what they could for the people. Many of them sacrificed their lives to duty, so much so that it was feared that the Order would die out. St. Peter Thomas loved his Order and our Lady dearly. He was stricken with grief at the thought that this might happen. While he was pleading with our Lady to preserve her Order, our Lady appeared to him and told him not to fear, that the Carmelite Order will last to the end of time. She said that Elijah, its ancient patron and father, had prayed for that on the day of the transfiguration, and Jesus had granted his petition.

With time and God's grace, the Order grew in number again. The Carmelites were able to spread throughout Europe once more.

In the sixteenth century, conditions in England became very trying for the Church. Henry VIII, at first a zealous, good king, who had defended his Faith, turned against his true wife and against the Pope. He made himself head of the Catholic Church in England. Whoever refused to recognize him as such he considered his enemy. Many martyrs received their crowns during this time, among them many Carmelites. Monasteries were plundered or confiscated.

In 1538, perceiving what was happening, the Carmelites at Aylesford fled in time. The Aylesford property was taken by the Crown and was given to Sir Thomas Wyatt, who lived at Allington Castle. Later, Elizabeth I gave it to Sir John Sedley of Southfleet. It passed to different families in the course of the centuries.

The beautiful Church of the Assumption was demolished and the stones were used, it is believed, to build a bridge over the River Medway. The hermitage was boarded up and used as a stable. A tower gate was built and various improvements were made, but the monastery was not destroyed.

The Protestant Reformation prevented the return of the Carmelites to England. In Ireland, the Carmelites maintained one house under trying conditions, but they did not give up. Through the Irish province, the work of the Carmelites was extended to America and to Australia.

In the early 1900's, after 400 years, the Carmelites returned to England—to Faversham, Kent, and on October 31, 1949, after an exile of 411 years, the Carmelites returned to their ancient priory at Aylesford. They had been able to purchase it. Repairs and improvements were begun at once. The boarded windows were located and soon the stables were reconverted into the hermitages they had once been.

Carpenters and artists worked diligently with the Carmelites in restoring the famous monastery buildings. Plans for the seventh centenary of the scapular vision were made.

On July 16, 1951, the seven-hundredth anniversary of the scapular vision was celebrated with great solemnity and dignity in Aylesford. On that day, some of the relics of St. Simon Stock were brought to Aylesford. St. Simon had died at the age of one hundred in Bordeaux, France, when he had been making a tour of the Carmelite houses. Through the centuries his body had been carefully preserved and honored in Bordeaux. Rededicated, Aylesford has again become a great Carmelite center.

Thousands of pilgrims have visited Aylesford. Weekend retreats are given, pilgrimages are made to it, and the work of spreading the faith and devotion to our Lady in England is again the zealous labor of the Carmelites. Allington Castle has become Carmelite property also.

The story of the scapular vision has come down to us by means of Carmelite tradition. The complete details of it are no longer known. Any authentic documents from St. Simon Stock concerning the apparition were destroyed. White Friars Hall in London had a wonderful library which was completely destroyed. The French Revolution caused the Carmelites to leave France. If any information was left in Bordeaux, where St. Simon Stock died, it was probably destroyed. The Sabbatine Privilege, as we have already mentioned, was issued by Pope John XXII who, at the time, resided in France. The Carmelites received the bull, and they still have it. Succeeding popes have confirmed the bull and sanctioned the teaching of the Sabbatine Privilege.

Heaven itself has backed up the scapular devotion by means of miracles not only in St. Simon's day, but through the centuries and even today. Through the scapular the dead have arisen, memories have been restored, fires have been extinguished, shipwrecks have been avoided, bullets have been flattened, swords have been blunted, sight has been restored, the sick have been cured, floods have been halted, the drowning have been rescued, souls have been converted and saved.

Some scapulars have been found perfectly preserved in the decay of tombs. Pope Gregory X died a few years after St. Simon Stock's death in the thirteenth century. In 1830, his remains were placed in a silver reliquary. A small purple silk scapular had been found lying over the Pope's shoulders in perfect preservation. Under their decayed garments, the scapulars of St. Alphonsus and St. John Bosco were found in perfect condition.

The popes through the ages have had personal love and devotion for the scapular. The two little tabs attached to strings do not matter so much as our Lady. She is all important. It is love for and consecration to Mary that matters. The scapular is an outward sign of that consecration, and it is the sign given by her. She loves it; she blesses it. So, too, does she love the devout wearer and she blesses him or her. Pope Leo XI recognized this. When his scapular was accidentally removed from him at the moment of his papal investiture, he said quickly, "Leave me Mary, so that Mary will not leave me!" As he saw death approaching, Pope Leo XIII called his friends and relatives to his bedside and said, "Let us make a novena to Our Lady of the Scapular and I shall be ready to die." Pope Pius XI said that he learned to love the Scapular Virgin in the arms of his mother.

In 1910, Pope St. Pius X recognized that circumstances existed which rendered the wearing of the cloth scapular inconvenient in some places. In his zeal that all men might avail themselves of the scapular benefits and our Lady's intercession throughout life and in death, he extended all scapular privileges, including the great Sabbatine Privilege, to the scapular medal, which has on one side an image of the Sacred Heart and on the other an image of our Lady. But he stated that he desired the cloth scapular to be worn wherever possible. Investiture requires the use of a cloth scapular; thereafter the scapular medal, blessed by a priest, may be worn or carried.

Pope Benedict XV declared in 1916, "To show it is our desire that the brown scapular be worn, we grant to it a grace that the scapular medal shall not enjoy." With that he granted an indulgence for each time the scapular is kissed.

On one July sixteenth, Pope Benedict XV, in addressing the seminarians of Rome, said, "Let all of you have the same language and the same armor—the language, the sentences of the Gospels; the same armor, the scapular of the Virgin of Carmel, which you all ought to wear and which brings the singular privilege of protection even after death."

The brown scapular is a Carmelite devotion, but since the Carmelites cannot be everywhere, they authorize priests to enroll members in the Scapular Confraternity. A priest obtains his faculties from the Carmelite Order or from the Holy See. He must love the scapular and wear it himself if he wants to lead others to love and wear it. One of the greatest works one can accomplish on this earth is the salvation of immortal souls. What an assurance Mary offers to a zealous priest—an assurance that anyone who dies clothed in a certain sign shall not die in mortal sin.

A zealous pastor once wrote: "So firmly do I believe in the fulfillment of the promise, that in every parish I established the Scapular Confraternity, I told the faithful, 'If your pastor knew that all his parishioners wore the scapular and died in it, he would be certain that we would meet again in heaven, without one exception.'"

Another holy priest said: "Since I have devoted myself to propagating the scapular in my parish, I have noticed that no one dies without the sacraments."

Our confidence and trust is not in the brown cloth. Our confidence and trust is in the intercession of the powerful Mother of God, who has made a promise and who is able to keep that promise. In wearing the scapular, we dedicate, we consecrate ourselves to our Lady, whose love for us prompted her gift.

Our Lady's last visit to Bernadette at Lourdes was on July sixteenth, the feastday of Our Lady of Mount Carmel. Bernadette said that Mary had never looked so beautiful as she did then. The last vision at Fatima as seen by Lucy on October thirteenth was of Our Lady of Mount Carmel. Lucy said that she understood by that apparition that the rosary and the scapular are inseparable. Through the scapular we consecrate ourselves to

Mary. We wear her livery, her garment, to honor her, to show our love for her. True love leads to imitation. So we can best show our honor and our love for Mary by imitating her, by being like her. In trying to imitate her who was a perfect imitator of her divine Son, we become more pleasing to God, and we draw closer to him on the path of holiness. Mary will then be with us at death, and her loving hands will reach out in purgatory to take us to heaven.

VII

Our Lady of the Snows

The sparkling crystals of the snow
Shone in the August sun;
They melted not, but beamed so bright
To praise what you had done.
They waited for your sceptered bow,
And disappeared by heaven's will;
The awe-struck Romans raised a gem
Upon your chosen hill.
You grace the niche, you grace the nave,
Supreme doth reign your Son;
The Queen of heaven and earth are you—
Your crown so nobly won.

In the fourth century a devout couple lived in Rome. The man's name was John. History does not give his wife's name. They were blessed with much wealth and deep faith, but to their sorrow, they had no children with whom to share their wealth and faith. For years they had prayed for a son and heir, or for a daughter to whom they could leave their fortune. Years had passed, but heaven seemed deaf to their prayer.

John and his wife decided that since they were getting old, they would make our Lady their heiress. They prayed devoutly to her, begging her to show them how she wanted to use her inheritance.

On the night of August fourth, our Lady appeared to John and his wife, telling them she wanted a basilica built on the Esquiline hill, on the exact spot that she would designate with snow. Our Lady also appeared to Pope Liberius, giving him the same information.

The next morning, August fifth, people were surprised to see a snowy carpet, sparkling in the sun, on the Esquiline, one of Rome's seven hills. The happy couple rushed to the spot. Pope Liberius marched to it with a solemn procession. The snow covered the exact space to be used for the basilica. After the site had been staked off, the snow disappeared.

The construction of the basilica began at once, the Pope giving the first stroke of the pickax in digging the foundation. The generous people watched excitedly as their gift to our Lady went up. Pope Liberius consecrated our Lady's shrine in A.D. 360.

It was and it still is the largest Roman church dedicated to our Lady. Because of its great size and unusual splendor, it received the name St. Mary Major or Greater. It is also known as the church of St. Mary of the Snows because of the miracle which is commemorated in mosaic above the doorway. A third name for it is the Liberian

Basilica, in memory of Pope Liberius who consecrated it. Another title for it is the Church of St. Mary of the Crib, because the basilica preserves what is believed to be a part of the crib of the Infant Jesus brought to Rome by St. Helena.

St. Helena had also brought to Rome a beautiful image of our Lady and the divine Child, supposedly painted by St. Luke on a thick cedar slab nearly five feet high and three and a quarter feet wide. This picture had been placed in the papal chapel for veneration.

Pope Liberius wanted an image of Mary worthy of the magnificent Basilica of St. Mary Major. He thought of this famous Madonna of St. Luke and generously gave it to the shrine.

Throughout the years, the people of Rome have had a great devotion to Mary. Whenever Rome was in danger from calamities or pestilence, the people would flock to our Lady's shrine, pleading for help. The image would be devoutly carried around in solemn procession. Our Lady proved herself a powerful protectress. Many wonderful miracles took place. Today the picture is called Our Lady, Protectress of Rome or Help of the Roman People—*Salus Populi Romani*. Some of the copies made from this picture have themselves become miraculous. This is especially true of the one owned by the Jesuits.

The popes have always had a tender devotion for this famous picture of our Lady. Some of them spent whole nights in prayer before it. Benedict XIV made it a point to be present for the singing of the litanies in St. Mary Major on Saturdays. Paul V, on the eve of his death, expressed the desire to be carried to our Lady's chapel so he could die at her feet.

Since St. Mary Major serves as a second cathedral for the Bishop of Rome, the popes have often said Mass there.

Through the centuries, the popes considered it an honor and a privilege to beautify and adorn Mary's basilica. The original character of the basilica has been preserved, notwithstanding the many decorations and improvements added. The mosaics in the chancel arch and on the walls of the nave are among the finest in Rome. They depict scenes in the life of our Lady. The beautiful ceiling is decorated with the first gold brought from America by Columbus. The Blessed Sacrament Chapel constructed by Sixtus V is one of the most magnificent in Rome. The Pauline or Borghese Chapel was built by Paul V as a throne room for our Lady's picture. The wealth of marble and precious stones in the chapel make it the richest in all the city. It is considered one of the best monuments of the sixteenth century. The facade or front of St. Mary Major is an eighteenth century addition. This shrine of our Lady is considered the greatest in Italy after that of Loreto and is the chief of all churches dedicated to the Mother of God.

The feast of our Lady of the Snows was at first celebrated only at the basilica. In the fourteenth century it was extended to the whole of Rome. St. Pius V made it a feast of the universal Church in the seventeenth century. Each year, on August fifth, the anniversary of the origin of St. Mary Major is celebrated with much splendor. The Pauline Chapel is beautifully illuminated and decorated. During the more solemn Masses a shower of white rose petals is released from the ceiling. It is a symbol of the miraculous fall of snow that indicated the site and size of the basilica. It also symbolizes the grace the Mother of God has bestowed on her children as well as the graces she continues to bestow. It is a touching custom that has always impressed the spectators.

On November 1, 1954, at the end of the Marian Year, the Holy Father placed a jeweled crown on the painting of Our Lady, Protectress of Rome. As he did so a great cry arose from the vast crowd assembled in St. Mary Major: "Long live the Queen!" The Pope then named Mary the Queen of heaven and earth and declared that a special feast would honor her under that title.

It was not a new belief or a new privilege for Mary. Mary has always been considered our Queen, as our statues, our pictures, our prayers, and especially the Litany of Loreto, can prove. But there was no particular feast commemorating this. Now August 22 is the day on which the Church honors Mary's Queenship. It was proclaimed in Mary's basilica, the Church of Our Lady of the Snows.

+O.L. of LA SALETTE+

IN MEMORY OF
SABATINO AND GRAZIA
PITOCHELLI

VIII

Our Lady of La Salette

"Why do you weep, O Lady?
Why do you weep?"
"The hand of my Son grows heavy;
I fear it is too late,
I cannot hold it back any more
I must leave you to your fate."
Maximin and Melanie, in fear,
Stood before the Lady fair.
They heard the warning given,
The need for penance and prayer.
They told the country's people
What they had seen and heard.
Some doubted; some believed,
And took them at their word.
Many profited by that message
Given them for us.
It *still* holds true today—
In Mary let us trust.

Once on a high mountainous plateau in southeast-
ern France near La Salette, a little boy, Maximin Giraud,
eleven years old, and a girl, Melanie Mathieu, fifteen,
were tending cows. Melanie had been accustomed to this
work since she was nine. But this was new work for
Maximin. His father had asked him to do it as an act of
kindness for a farmer friend whose helper was ill at the
time.

On this particular day, a Saturday, September 19,
1846, the two children found it very hot and agreed to eat
lunch together in a shady spot. Then they drove the
cows to drink at a stream. Finding a cool spot, a dried-up
spring, they decided to stretch out for a nap. Both slept
soundly.

Melanie was the first to waken. She missed the
cows, so she quickly called Maximin. Together they
climbed up the plateau and looked around. The animals
were grazing peacefully below. The two children then
decided to go back for their lunch bags before descending to the cows. Looking toward the spring near where
they had been sleeping, they saw a luminous globe. This
globe of light seemed to divide, and they saw a Lady
seated on a large rock. She had her face in her hands, and
she was weeping bitterly. The two children were very
afraid. The Lady slowly stood up, crossed her arms, and
called them to her, telling them not to be frightened. She
added that she had some important news to tell them.
She was so beautiful that the children no longer feared
her. They went very near.

The Lady was tall and stately. She wore a long,
white dress with a golden apron tied at the waist. Her
white shawl was bordered with roses of different colors.
Her white shoes were bordered with the same many-
colored roses. Around her neck hung a chain with a
crucifix. From the crossbar of the crucifix hung a ham-

mer and a pincers. A crown of roses radiated bright rays like a diadem. From the Lady's beautiful eyes tears ran down her cheeks. The light that surrounded her was brighter than the sun, but different.

She told the children that the hand of her Son was so strong and heavy that she could no longer hold it back, and that unless people did penance and obeyed God's law they would have much to suffer. The people were not observing the Lord's Day; they continued to work on Sunday. Only a few old ladies went to Mass in the summer. In winter, when they had nothing else to do, the boys went to Mass just to mock religion. Lent was ignored. The men could not swear without taking the Lord's name in vain. Disobedience and disregard for God's commandments were the things that made her Son's hand so heavy.

The Lady went on to predict a terrible famine. She told them that the potato crop had been poor the year before for that reason. When the men found the potatoes spoiled, they swore and blasphemed her Son's name all the more. Now she said that the potato crop would be a complete failure. Corn and wheat would turn to dust when threshed. The nut crop would go bad, and the grapes would rot. She then confided to each child a secret which they revealed to no one—except later to the Pope at his special request.

The Lady stated that if the people were converted, the very rocks and stones would turn to grain, and the potatoes would be self-sown for another year.

She then asked the children if they said their prayers well. When they answered, "Not very well," she told them to say them carefully every morning and every night, never less than an "Our Father" and a "Hail Mary" when they could do no better.

Then, in a concerned motherly voice, the Lady said, "Well, my children, you will make this known to all my people." Then she was raised about five feet from the earth and was slowly absorbed into the shining light which surrounded her. Like a second sun, the globe of light rose and disappeared into the sky.

At first hardly anyone wanted to believe the children when they told what they had seen and heard. The farmers who had hired them were astonished that such ignorant children were able to relate so complicated a message both in French, which they did not understand, and in their dialect, which showed the exactness of what they said.

The very next morning the children were taken to see the parish priest. He was a kind-hearted, venerable old man who questioned them carefully. He listened to what they related and felt that they were telling the truth. At his Sunday Mass, he told the people of our Lady's visit and of her requests. He was very impressed by it.

The Church is very slow and cautious in passing judgment on such matters. When the bishop heard that the pastor had spoken of this from the pulpit, he reprimanded the pastor and sent another priest to replace him.

The children were questioned by the curious and by the devout. They readily and simply told their story, repeating it over and over. To those who were interested enough to climb the mountainous plateau, they pointed out the spot where our Lady had appeared. The city officials threatened the children with imprisonment if they did not take back what they were saying. But the two children fearlessly continued to report accurately and without hesitation all that our Lady had said. The spring near to the place where our Lady sat had begun to gush water, which flowed freely down the hill. Many miracles began to take place.

The terrible calamities predicted took place. The potato famine of 1846 was widespread and terrible. The wheat and corn shortage was so severe that more than a million people in Europe died of starvation. A grape disease affected the vineyards all over France. The punishment would probably have been worse except for the fact that many people heeded the message of La Salette. They began going to church in large numbers. Cursing and swearing became less common. The shops were closed on Sundays, and people stopped doing unnecessary work on that day.

The bishop appointed two commissioners to investigate the apparition and the cures. For five years they made the most searching inquiries. All over France in as many as eighty places, bishops appointed commissioners who gave judgment that cures granted through prayers to Our Lady of La Salette and use of water from the spring were miraculous. Hundreds of remarkable favors were recorded.

Pope Pius IX, approved the devotion to Our Lady of La Salette. He asked the children to write down the secrets and send them to him. He later exclaimed: "These are the secrets of La Salette: Unless the world repent, it shall perish!"

A magnificent basilica was built on the site of the apparition, 6,000 feet above sea level. Hospices were erected nearby for the convenience and welfare of pilgrims. A new congregation of priests was founded—the Priest Missionaries of Our Lady of La Salette. They now have houses and colleges in many parts of the world. To further their work and to assist in spreading our Lady's message of penance, a confraternity was founded. It was raised almost instantly to the status of an arch-confraternity. A congregation of religious, the Sisters of Our Lady of La Salette, was established to aid the women pilgrims and the sick. Many pilgrimages are made yearly to the basilica. Thousands of pilgrims, in a spirit of penance, climb to the mountain plateau. Many miracles are still being worked for soul and body, depending on the devotion of the faithful and the grace of God.

Maximin tried to become a priest. He entered the minor seminary but had much difficulty in learning, and did not have the qualities needed for the priesthood. He was dismissed. He worked in a hospital for a while, became a soldier, and finally operated a small shop, selling religious articles. Some unscrupulous persons tried to take advantage of him as a seer of Mary; he made a number of mistakes, but he lived a good life. He died a holy death when he was thirty-eight years old.

Melanie tried to become a sister. She entered several communities, but was unable to remain long in any of them. She did not have the qualifications for community life. She lived a model Christian life in the world, enduring poverty, hardships and misunderstandings. She died a holy death in Italy at the age of seventy-three.

The message of Our Lady of La Salette, given to Maximin and Melanie for the world in 1846, is still an important message today—to avoid sin and to do penance, or terrible trials and sufferings will come upon the world. That was also our Lady's message at Lourdes and Fatima—prayer, penance, consecration.

IX

Our Lady of the Rosary

Faith, hope and charity on wings of prayer
Knelt before the Queen.
They told her of the plight of man,
And the horrors they had seen.
They told of Dominic and his need
Of a weapon, bold and true,
To touch the hearts of misled men,
And a burning faith renew.
The Queen smiled, a sad, sweet smile.
How well she knew mankind!
What wisdom Dominic had displayed;
Better messengers he ne'er could find.
The Queen and her Son, with seraphs three
Laden with roses fair,
Before an astonished Dominic stood
In answer to his prayer.
Three chains of love the Queen gave him
With the roses intertwined,
The white, the red, the gold—
And the lessons he divined.
The joyful mysteries of Mother and Son,
A chaplet of delight
He saw in the "Paters" and "Aves"
Of the lovely roses white.
In the heart of the blood red roses
He saw a thorn-crowned king;
Of the five sorrowful mysteries
The "Paters" and "Aves" did sing.
A diadem fair saw he
In the gorgeous roses of gold.
The glorious mysteries bespoke triumph,
Which the "Paters" and "Aves" retold.
Thought and prayer, mind and heart,
Together they had to be.
'Twas indeed a victorious weapon
From Our Lady of the Rosary.

In 1208, the great Mother of God herself taught St. Dominic how to say the rosary and told him to spread its devotion and to use it as his powerful weapon against the enemies of the Faith.

Dominic de Guzman was a holy, zealous Spanish priest who had come to southern France to convert people who had fallen into error. The Albigensian heresy had caused many people to give up their Catholic Faith and to adopt a gloomy, frightful one which taught that there are two gods, a god of good and a god of evil. The good one made all that is spiritual. The evil one made all that is material. So to these people all material things were bad. The body is material; therefore the body is bad. Jesus had a body, so Jesus was not God. They also denied the sacraments and the truth that Mary is the Mother of God. They refused to recognize the Pope and set up their own norms of belief. For years the popes sent zealous priests to try to convert them, but they were unable to do so. Political factors were also involved.

Dominic labored among these unfortunate people for years. Through his preaching, prayers and sacrifices, he was able to convert a few. But so often because of ridicule and hardships, the converts would give up. Dominic started a religious order for the young women he converted. Their convent was next to a chapel dedicated to our Lady. It was in this chapel that Dominic pleaded with our Lady for help, for he felt he was making such little headway. Our Lady then appeared to him. She held a rosary in her hand, taught Dominic how to say it, and told him to preach it to the world, promising that many sinners would be converted and many graces obtained.

Dominic went out full of zeal with the rosary in his hand. He preached it and successfully brought many of the Albigensians back to the Catholic Faith.

In the military crusade fought against some of these people who had taken up arms, the rosary played an important part. Simon de Montfort, the leader of the Christian army and a great friend of Dominic, had his soldiers instructed by Dominic as to how to say the rosary. They recited it devoutly before their most important battle at Muret. De Montfort considered their victory a miracle and the result of the rosary. In gratitude, De Montfort built the first chapel to Our Lady of the Rosary.

Gradually, a number of men began to join Dominic in his great apostolic work. With the Holy Father's approval, Dominic formed the Order of Preachers or Dominicans. They zealously went around preaching, teaching and converting. As the Order grew, they went to different countries working for the glory of God and our Lady.

The rosary remained a favorite devotion of Christians for nearly two centuries. Later, when devotion to the rosary seemed to slacken, our Lady appeared to Blessed Alan de la Roche and told him to revive devotion to the rosary. She said that immense volumes would be needed to record all its miracles. She had made a number of promises to St. Dominic concerning the rosary. To Blessed Alan, also, she made promises.

The following promises of our Lady, Queen of the Rosary, to St. Dominic and Blessed Alan are taken from the writings of Blessed Alan:

1. Whoever will faithfully serve me by the recitation of the rosary shall receive extraordinary graces.

2. I promise my special protection and great graces to all who recite my rosary devoutly.

3. The rosary will be a very powerful armor against hell. It will destroy vice, deliver from sin, and dispel heresy.

4. The rosary will make virtue and good works flourish, and will obtain the most abundant divine mercies for mankind; it will substitute in hearts love of God for love of the world and will elevate people to desire heavenly and eternal goods. Oh, that souls would sanctify themselves by this means!

5. Those who entrust themselves to me through the rosary will not perish.

6. Those who shall recite my rosary prayerfully, considering its mysteries, will not be overwhelmed by misfortune, or die a bad death. The sinner will be converted, the just will grow in grace and become worthy of eternal life.

7. Whoever will have a true devotion for the rosary shall not die without the sacraments of the Church.

8. Those who faithfully recite the rosary shall have during their life and at their death the light of God and the plenitude of his graces. At the moment of death they shall participate in the merits of the saints in paradise.

9. I will deliver promptly from purgatory the souls devoted to my rosary.

10. The true children of my rosary will enjoy great glory in heaven.

11. What you shall ask through the rosary you shall obtain.

12. All those who propagate the holy rosary shall be aided by me in their necessities.

13. I have obtained from my divine Son that all the advocates of the rosary shall have for intercessors the entire celestial court during their life and at the hour of death.

14. All who recite the rosary are my children, and brothers and sisters of my only Son Jesus Christ.

15. Devotion to my rosary is a great sign of predestination.

The spread of devotion to the rosary was given as a special charge by St. Pius V, the great holy Dominican Pope, to the Order of Preachers. It is still their special charge and great devotion.

For centuries there had been a conflict between the Catholic powers of Europe and the Turks, the followers of Mohammed. The Mohammedans had captured the Holy Land, Constantinople, Greece, Albania, North Africa and Spain. They had been gradually driven out of Spain by Ferdinand and Isabella.

In the time of Pope Pius V, the Mohammedans still had control of the Mediterranean Sea and threatened to overrun Christian Europe. The Catholic powers of Europe were quarreling among themselves and did not seem to realize the danger from the invading Turks. The Pope appealed for help, but little seemed to be forthcoming.

On September 17, 1569, the Pope enjoined the recitation of the rosary on all Christendom for the success of the Christian forces against the Turks. The papal soldiers, aided by soldiers from Venice, Genoa and Spain, and commanded by Don Juan of Austria, sailed for the Ionian Sea. They went up the Gulf of Corinth, and near Lepanto, a town in Greece, they fought the Turkish fleet. Before the attack, the Christians had devoutly recited the rosary. On October 7, 1571, the battle raged until late afternoon.

In Rome, the Pope and his household were reciting the rosary as the decisive and miraculous victory was won by the Christians. The power of the Turks on the sea was broken forever and Christendom was saved. Inspired, the Pope left his chapel and calmly told the people that our Lady had given the Christians the victory.

It was some weeks before the actual message of victory arrived from Don Juan. From the very first, Don Juan attributed the triumph of his fleet to the powerful intercession of Our Lady of the Rosary. In gratitude to our Lady, Pope Pius V instituted the feast of Our Lady of Victory and added the title "Help of Christians" to the Litany of the Blessed Virgin. Later, Pope Gregory XIII renamed the feast, Our Lady of the Rosary.

The Battle of Lepanto broke the sea power of the Turks, but they were still powerful on land. In the following century, they invaded Hungary and laid siege to the capital of Austria, Vienna, before the Austrian army had time to completely mobilize. There was much fighting and bloodshed, but the emperor placed his hope in Our Lady of the Rosary. Relief came on the feast of the Holy Name of Mary, September 12, 1683, when the King of Poland, leading a rescue army, defeated the Turks.

The Turks suffered another great defeat at the hands of Prince Eugene of Savoy, the commander of the Christian armies, at Temesvar in modern Rumania, on August 5, 1716, the feast of Our Lady of Snow. Pope Clement XI attributed this victory to the devotion shown to Our Lady of the Rosary. In gratitude he commanded that the feast of the Holy Rosary be celebrated by the universal Church.

Through the centuries the popes have encouraged the devout recitation of the rosary. They have attached many indulgences to it. "A *plenary indulgence* is granted if the rosary is recited in a church or public oratory or in a family group, a religious community or pious association; a *partial indulgence* is granted in other circumstances" (Enchiridion of Indulgences, p. 67).

Our Lord has said: "Where two or three are gathered in my name, there I am in their midst" (Mt 18:20). The family rosary is a wonderful thing. It is a practical way to strengthen the unity of family life. The popes, especially of recent years, have pleaded for the family rosary.

Pope Leo XIII wrote twelve encyclicals on the rosary. Because of his love for our Lady and her rosary and because of his efforts in furthering devotion to the rosary, he has been called the Pope of the rosary. He consecrated the month of October to the rosary, and he inserted the title "Queen of the Most Holy Rosary" in the Litany of the Blessed Virgin. He and the other popes before and after him have preached the family rosary by word and example.

Another great apostle of the family rosary was Father Patrick Peyton. He made the first plans for a worldwide crusade for the family rosary at Holy Cross College, Washington, D.C., in January 1942. He took up this crusade in thanksgiving to our Lady for the restoration of his health. Through the use of the press, radio, television, rallies and travel, Father Peyton was able to spread his message throughout the world: "The family that prays together stays together." He has been able to effectively teach and preach the family rosary.

The rosary is such a perfect prayer. It combines the most sublime of vocal prayers with meditation. It begins with the Sign of the Cross, the sign of our Redemption. Next comes the "Apostles' Creed," a prayer that contains all the truths and mysteries of our Catholic Faith. The "Our Father," composed by our Lord himself, is a prayer full of meaning and power, a summary of the Gospel. The "Hail Mary," the angel's greeting to Mary and that of the church, is a prayer of love, praise and petition to

God's Mother and ours. The "Glory Be" gives praise to the Blessed Trinity.

Meditation is the most important part of the rosary. As we say the vocal prayers, we think about the chief mysteries of our Redemption. We fix our attention on the joyful mysteries, the sorrowful mysteries, or the glorious mysteries. According to tradition, this is the part of the rosary which our Lady took such care to explain to St. Dominic. It is by thinking of Christ—his joys, sorrows and triumphs—that we begin to appreciate more what he has done for us, that we begin to love him more and more and imitate him more. We begin to understand, too, the role Mary has played in our Redemption. The mysteries of the rosary bring us closer to Jesus and to Mary.

Our Lady loves the rosary. It is the prayer of the simple and of the great. Everyone can so easily pray it anywhere, any time. It honors God and our Lady in a special way. When our Lady appeared to Bernadette at Lourdes, she had a rosary in her hand. When she appeared to the three children of Fatima, she also held a rosary. It was at Fatima that she definitely called herself by the title she dearly loves, "The Lady of the Rosary."

MIRACULOUS MEDAL

X

Our Lady of the Miraculous Medal

It is only an oval medallion
But a symbol of Mary's love.
She gave it for us to St. Catherine—
A source of blessings from above.
All graces come to us through Mary;
Jesus himself wills it that way.
He tenderly loves his dear Mother
And will do what she chooses to say.
Mary's love for God is so perfect;
She wants our love for him to be strong,
For love is proved by words and by actions
And by courageously singing life's song,
The song of love, of praise, of valorous deeds
For God and for God alone
As we joyously walk the path of duty,
Lifting hearts besides our own.
Mary wants us to pray for our blessings,
To be grateful to God for all things,
And so she gives us a reminder—
A token—a medal with wings,
For faithfully to wear the medal
Is a symbol of love and of praise
And a silent prayer of intercession
Which we to our Mother do raise.
Her hands are outstretched with blessings
For all of her children so true.
Call on her sincerely today;
She has countless favors for you.

In a little country village in France, Fain-les-moutiers in Burgundy, lived a hard-working farmer named Peter Labouré. He had a very devout wife and eleven active, happy children, eight boys and three girls. Zoé was the ninth of this group.

When Zoé was nine years old, her mother died. The girl took this hard; she loved her mother very much. Mrs. Labouré had taught her children to love our Lady greatly. She had tried to make them realize that the Mother of God was their heavenly Mother, also. This had impressed Zoé. When she lost her own dear mother, Zoé turned to our Lady with a deeper devotion, asking her to be truly her Mother. Her devotion deepened with the years.

Shortly after her mother's death, Zoé's Aunt Margaret, her father's sister, decided to take the two younger girls under her maternal care. So Zoé and her younger sister, Marie Antoinette, went to live with her. They stayed with their aunt for two years; then their father brought them home. He needed them to help him manage the house because his oldest daughter was planning to become a Sister of Charity.

Zoé was happy to be back home. She and Marie Antoinette set to work in the large farm house to make their father and brothers happy. Zoé kneaded the bread, did the washing, and carried the meals to the men working in the fields. She enjoyed caring for and feeding the eight hundred pigeons her father owned. The massive dove-cote still stands today.

When Zoé was twelve, she made her First Communion. From this time on, she felt a desire to consecrate herself to God. Often on weekdays, early in the morning, she walked a mile and a half to the next village to attend Mass either in the church or in the hospice which was under the care of the Sisters of Charity. Gradually the desire to serve God in the religious life began to take possession of her.

Being a dutiful daughter, Zoé waited with secret impatience until her younger sister would be old enough to take charge of the house. She began to undertake severe penances, fasting on Fridays and Saturdays, even when her work was heavy. Throughout her well-filled day, she often had recourse to prayer.

Several times Zoé's hand was asked in marriage, but each time she refused. She wished for no other spouse but Jesus.

One night she had a dream which made a deep impression on her. She found herself in the village church. An old priest appeared and said Mass, at which she devoutly assisted. At the end of the Mass, he made the sign for her to approach, but she fearfully drew back. On leaving the church, she went to visit a sick person. She found the old priest there. He said to her: "My child, it is a good deed to visit the sick. You run away from me now, but one day you will be happy to come to me. God has his designs upon you. Do not forget it." Then she woke up. Zoé never forgot that dream and the old priest.

When Zoé was twenty-two, she felt that her sister was capable of replacing her. She asked her father's permission to become a sister. He emphatically forbade her to do so. He had given one daughter to the Church, and the thought that Zoé, his favorite, would leave him forever was something he could not bear. Zoé suffered in silence and begged God to take things in hand for her.

In order to distract her and perhaps to change her ideas, Zoé's father decided to send her away from the farm. He sent her to Paris with her brother Charles, who owned a restaurant. Zoé knew that God would not abandon her in a Paris restaurant. She stayed one year with

Charles, bearing this hard trial as uncomplainingly as she could. She was miserable and out of place. When her sister-in-law, Mrs. Hubert Labouré, visited her in Paris, she noted this. She asked if she could bring Zoé to her home at Chatillon, where she conducted a boarding school. Here poor Zoé felt just as out of place, for the fashionable young ladies attending the Labouré school looked down on the uneducated peasant girl.

Hubert's wife was kind, tactful and farsighted. She wholeheartedly adopted Zoé's cause. She took Zoé to visit the Sisters of Charity in Chatillon. On entering the parlor Zoé was astonished to see a picture, the perfect portrait of the old priest in her dream. When she asked who he was, she was told that he was the founder of the Sisters of Charity, St. Vincent de Paul. Her desire to become a Sister of Charity grew stronger than ever.

Mrs. Hubert Labouré finally persuaded Zoé's father to give his consent. She herself gave the money required as a dowry by the community, and she saw Zoé enter as a postulant at the house of the Sisters of Charity in Chatillon.

After a three month's test, Zoé left for Paris to begin her novitiate at the motherhouse at 140 Rue du Bac. She was given the name Sister Catherine. Her devotion and piety increased. She was humble, sincere and hard-working.

During the night of July 18, 1830, Sister Catherine was awakened by hearing her name called three times in succession. To her great surprise, she saw a beautiful child of about four or five years of age. He was dressed in white, and rays of light issued from his entire person. "Come," he said. "Come to the chapel; the Blessed Virgin is waiting for you."

Sister Catherine sat up in bed, astonished but troubled. She slept in a large dormitory. The child reassured her: "Do not be afraid. It is half-past eleven and everyone is asleep. I will go with you."

Sister Catherine dressed quickly and followed her little guide, who kept always to the left side. The corridors were all brightly lighted, and, at the mere touch of the child's hand, the massive locked doors of the chapel opened. The chapel was brilliantly lighted. The candles on the altar, all burning brightly, reminded Sister Catherine of midnight Mass. She knelt at the altar rail and waited. Time seemed endless!

Toward midnight the child said, "The Blessed Virgin is coming. Here she is." Sister Catherine heard the rustling of silk as a beautiful Lady walked into the sanctuary and seated herself in an armchair. Following the impulse of her heart, Sister Catherine threw herself at our Lady's feet, confidently resting her hands on Mary's knees. There, she later said, she spent the sweetest moments of her life.

Mary instructed her as to how she was to act in moments of trial, in pointing to the altar, she told her that she would receive there all the consolations necessary for her. Our Lady predicted that terrible misfortunes were about to fall on France, that the throne would be overturned, and the entire world would be afflicted by misery of some kind. There would be great danger then and forty years later, but the community would be protected by God and St. Vincent. Our Lady also told her that God had a special mission to confide to her. She would suffer many trials and contradictions, but she would be given the grace, so she was not to fear. After talking to Sister Catherine for a long time, our Lady withdrew and slowly disappeared. The child led Sister Catherine back to her dormitory, and as she was getting back into bed, a distant clock struck two.

Shortly after this—in fact, within a few days—the terrible Revolution of 1830 broke out. There was bloodshed and disaster for France. It did not last long, but it was terrible. Our Lady had predicted that a worse disaster would take place in forty years. In 1870, the Franco-Prussian War caused much more trouble for France and for the Church.

Sister Catherine was instructed to tell no one about her visitor except her confessor. She told him everything except personal secrets confided to her by our Lady.

Our Lady had not told Sister Catherine what her special mission would be. She had come to prepare her for it. Sister Catherine found out what it was on November twenty-seventh.

The sisters were all assembled in the chapel making their evening meditation. There was absolute silence. Sister Catherine heard the rustle of silk. Looking in the direction from which the sound came, she beheld our Lady. Mary was dressed in a shining white robe, a sky blue mantle, and a white veil. She was standing on a globe, her feet crushing the serpent. In her hands, she held a smaller globe which she seemed to offer to God. Suddenly her fingers were filled with jeweled rings, three on each finger. The brilliant rays that gleamed from the gems reflected on all sides.

As Sister Catherine was absorbed in what she saw, our Lady lowered her eyes on her and a voice said in the depths of her heart: "The globe that you see represents the entire world, especially France and each person in particular." Then the small globe disappeared and our Lady extended her radiant hands, saying: "Behold the symbol of graces I shed upon those who ask me for them." Then Sister Catherine understood how generous our Lady is to those who pray, how many graces she obtains for those who ask for them, and what a joy it is for our Lady to bestow them.

There now formed around the Blessed Virgin an oval shaped frame upon which appeared in letters of gold these words: "O Mary, conceived without sin, pray for us who have recourse to you!" Then Sister Catherine heard a voice: "Have a medal struck upon this model. All who wear it will receive great graces. Graces will be bestowed abundantly on those who have confidence." Suddenly the picture seemed to turn, and Catherine saw the reverse side. The letter M was surmounted by a cross with a bar at its base. Beneath the M were two hearts, one encircled by a crown of thorns and the other pierced with a sword. Twelve stars encircled this.

Sister Catherine was later asked what words were to be inscribed on the back of the medal. She asked our Lady, who told her that the M with the cross, the two hearts, and the stars say enough.

Sister Catherine immediately told Father Aladel, her confessor, about the apparition and the medal. This apparition appeared several times in the course of a few months, always in the chapel, either during Mass or during some of the religious exercises.

Months passed and the medal was not made. An interior voice soon reproached Sister Catherine. She knew that our Lady was not pleased. She told our Lady that Father Aladel did not believe her. Our Lady replied that she need not worry, that a day would come when he would do as she desired because he would fear to displease her.

When Father Aladel was told this, he knew that our Lady was not displeased with Sister Catherine but with him. He decided to act. Two years later, with the approval of the Archbishop of Paris, the medal of the Immaculate Conception was struck.

Medals were given out far and wide. So many cures and startling conversions resulted that people began to call the medal "Miraculous." The archbishop ordered a canonical investigation made in reference to the origin and the effects of the medal because of the extraordinary and astonishing benefits derived from it. Today the medal is known and worn on every continent, and it still works marvels of grace through Mary's help. It is her gift to us, reminding us of her presence and love.

The principal end of our Lady's apparitions to Sister Catherine was to develop devotion to the Immaculate Conception, and the medal was a means to this end. In 1830, through Sister Catherine, our Lady had sent Father Aladel a special message. The Blessed Virgin wanted Father to found a confraternity of Children of Mary. Many blessings would be bestowed upon it. The month of Mary, May, would be celebrated with more solemnity. Father was puzzled about this. He knew that sodalities of the Children of Mary already existed among the boys educated by the Jesuits, and that the Ladies of the Sacred Heart had formed similar associations among their pupils.

The more he pondered our Lady's request, the more he realized that these sodalities were confined to a few isolated places and to a chosen class. Mary wanted this for the multitude of young boys and girls in the ordinary walks of life, surrounded by all the trials and dangers of the world. He was not too sure how to go about getting such a confraternity started. He used every opportunity he could to speak to the children and young people of our Lady's goodness and of the joy of belonging to her. God blessed his work. His listeners were affected by his words, and trial associations were formed in the orphanages and schools conducted by the Sisters of Charity.

Approval was obtained from the Holy Father to establish in the schools of the Sisters of Charity the pious confraternity under the title of the Immaculate Conception of the most Blessed Virgin, with all the indulgences accorded the Sodality of the Children of Mary established at Rome for the Jesuit students.

From this time, the Confraternity or Sodality of the Children of Mary spread rapidly in all quarters of the globe. A manual containing rules of the association, its privileges and obligations, was written by Father Aladel. The livery adopted by the Children of Mary was the miraculous medal suspended by a blue ribbon.

The sodalities had wonderful results. Piety and devotion increased in imitation of and love for our Lady. Parish priests, the world over, began to know of the Sodality and its effects. They adopted it for their own people, young and old.

Many sodalities in the United States have become directly affiliated with the Jesuit sodality in Rome. Great Jesuits, like Father Daniel A. Lord, were very active in promoting greater love and devotion to our Lady by means of the parish sodalities, by *The Queen's Work,* a sodality magazine, by pamphlets and books, and by regional sodality conventions and rallies held throughout the United States.

When Sister Catherine's novitiate training was completed, she was sent to serve in a home for the aged; the House of Enghien, in Paris. There for forty-six years she helped to look after the elderly who resided there. She was first placed in the kitchen. Amid the pots and pans she served God in his poor. She also had charge of the poultry yard. This must have reminded her of her childhood days back home on the farm. As the years passed, Sister Catherine, ever leading a life of humility and prayer, tenderly cared for and nursed the poor, distributing the miraculous medal to all whom she met.

No one knew that our Lady appeared to her except Father Aladel, her confessor, and he was not allowed to reveal it to anyone. When he died, Sister Catherine was left with no one who knew her story.

A beautiful statue of Our Lady of the Miraculous Medal, with her hands extended as seen on the medal, had been placed over the main altar in the motherhouse chapel. Sister Catherine had told Father Aladel that our Lady also wanted one of her holding the globe. Father Aladel had made the sketches and drawing but had died before having the statue made.

Sister Catherine was aging. She suffered from painful rheumatism, and was no longer able to nurse and care for her poor. She acted as doorkeeper, welcoming visitors, and mending the linens. Above all, she prayed. She was worried about our Lady's statue.

One day Sister Catherine surprised her superior by bursting into tears. When her superior asked the cause, Catherine said she would tell her the next day if our Lady would give the permission. The next day she told her superior the whole story of the apparitions concerning the medal and the statue. The superior promised that the statue would be made according to the drawings. Sister Catherine was happy. She died peacefully within that year on December 31, 1876, knowing that our Lady of the globe would soon be in the motherhouse chapel.

Sister Catherine was canonized by Pope Pius XII on July 27, 1947. St. Catherine Labouré's body, perfectly preserved, rests under the altar of our Lady of the globe in the motherhouse chapel in Paris. Because the altar has a glass front panel, her body can be seen and venerated by all. There she reposes, dressed in the habit of the Sisters of Charity, awaiting the resurrection day.

The motherhouse chapel has been remodeled and made beautiful with a splendid mural of the first apparition and with lovely mosaics of pastel colors, bringing out the beauty of the white statues. Everything is conducive to prayer and recollection. The chair upon which our Lady sat is carefully preserved and regarded as a priceless treasure. It is close to the spot where St. Catherine lies.

The feast of Our Lady of the Miraculous Medal is celebrated with great solemnity in the motherhouse chapel. On the very next day, St. Catherine Labouré's feast is celebrated there with great rejoicing.

Through a favored, humble daughter of St. Vincent de Paul, a Sister of Charity, our Lady made known her desire to bestow blessings and graces on those who ask for them. The medal is a symbol of Mary's love and a means for those who truly love Mary to show that love.

XI

Our Lady of Guadalupe

Heaven painted a picture
On earth's coarse fibers mean!
Heaven painted a picture
Of a motherly, celestial queen!
The hearts of men responded
To this ethereal magnet true,
And blest is the western hemisphere,
The past ages and the new.
The Indians and the Spaniards
Had reason to rejoice
As the gentle queen of heaven
Made America her choice
For rays of heavenly graces
To penetrate the souls of men;
The worship of the one true God
Has ever been since then.
May the hearts of all Americans
In praise be lifted high
For the maid who loves America
And her Son who chose to die
To set the souls of all men free
From the grasp of satan's snare;
The fearful serpent has been crushed
By the feet of the heavenly pair.
Let love and trust, penance and prayer
In the hearts of men hold sway
And Our Lady of Guadalupe reign
As queen of the U.S.A.
Of Mexico and of Canada, too,
And the Latin American states—
Our pan-American mother, then,
In heaven for each of us waits,
With arms outstretched and a welcoming smile
To lead us to God's throne;
For love and service here on earth
Make us forever God's own.

Mary, the Mother of God, tenderly loves her children the world over. It was her motherly love and compassion which caused her to work miracles in behalf of the poor Aztec Indians of Mexico and the Spanish who were trying to convert them.

Cortes, the Spanish invader, had conquered Montezuma's capital in Mexico. He had destroyed the pagan temples and ended human sacrifices. He had hoped that the Indians would be quickly converted to Christianity through the zealous efforts of the Franciscans who had accompanied him. But the Indians held back. For a while language had been a barrier. But there was more than that. There was also fear—fear of the conquerors and fear because of all that had been lost. When they were told of God and the Mother of God, the majority of the Indians shrugged their shoulders in doubt or disbelief. Only a few accepted Christianity.

Among the few was a poor Aztec who had been baptized Juan Diego. He was simple, good and kind. His wife, Maria Lucia, had also been baptized, but then death took her from him and Juan went to live with his uncle, Bernardino, who had also been converted.

One cold day, December 9, 1531, Juan Diego left his village early to attend Saturday Mass and catechism instruction in another village. When he reached the foot of Tepeyac Hill, which he had to climb, he stopped in amazement. Angelic music seemed to come from the top of the hill. He looked up and saw a luminous cloud encircled by a rainbow. The music suddenly stopped. Juan distinctly heard his name called out clearly and sweetly, "Juan, Juanito!" Amazed, Juan hurriedly ascended the hill, where from the bright cloud a beautiful Lady stepped out.

The Lady was majestic. Her dark hair and rather dark complexion made her look like a mixture of Indian and Spanish. Her pink dress was brocaded in gold, and the blue mantle, which also covered her head, was spangled with stars. On her head was a golden crown.

She called Juan her precious one and told him that for years, she, the Mother of God, had looked with compassion on her poor Indians, and that their sorrows and tears beat on her soul. She wanted Juan to go to the bishop and tell him it was her will that a temple be built in her honor on Tepeyac Hill. Juan hastened to obey his beautiful Lady.

When Juan arrived at the bishop's palace in Mexico City, the servants noticed his poor and humble appearance and tried to dismiss him by saying that the bishop was very busy. But Juan insisted. He had to wait almost all day. The bishop listened with kindness to Juan's story. He told Juan to come back another day, and that he, in the meantime, would consider what he had been told. Juan left the palace a bit disheartened. He felt that the bishop did not understand or believe him.

Slowly Juan trudged homeward. When he reached Tepeyac Hill, our Lady was there waiting for him. He recounted the day's adventure and with tears besought our Lady to send a more worthy messenger, one who was smart and rich, one who could really impress the bishop. Our Lady told him that she had many messengers from whom she could pick, but she wanted Juan, and no other would do! She told him to return to the bishop the next day and to repeat her request.

The next day, Sunday, December tenth, Juan assisted at Mass and catechetical instructions, and then he went to the bishop's palace. The servants again made him wait a long time before they informed the bishop of his presence. When finally he did get to see the bishop, Juan, with tears and sighs, told him how our Lady, the Mother of God, had again appeared to him with the same request for a temple on Tepeyac. The bishop questioned Juan carefully. He was much impressed by Juan's sincerity and gentleness. He told Juan that in his position as bishop he needed more than Juan's words for what he was asking. He asked Juan to obtain from his Lady some sign to show that she was really the Mother of God.

When Juan left the palace, the bishop ordered two of his servants to follow and observe Juan closely. When Juan reached Tepeyac Hill, the servants lost sight of him completely. They searched around, and not finding him, they returned home, declaring that he was a sorcerer.

In the meantime, Juan met our Lady at the top of the hill. She listened to his account of the day. When he told her that the bishop wanted a sign, she smiled. She told him to return the next day, at which time she would give him a sign that would cause him to be received with joy.

When he returned home, Juan found his uncle very ill. He loved his uncle as a father. All night he sat beside him and cared for him. Since the old man was no better toward daybreak, Juan went for the doctor, who ordered medicine. Juan rushed off to get the medicine. All day he was so preoccupied with his uncle's needs that he found no time to think of our Lady's promised sign. That night Bernardino's condition was so grave that he felt his end was approaching and asked Juan to get a priest for him early the next morning.

Before daybreak on December twelfth, Juan was headed for the village to get a priest. At the sight of Tepeyac Hill, Juan realized that he had not fulfilled our Lady's request to return for the sign. Fearing that his uncle might die without the priest if he were detained, Juan took another road. He planned to return to our Lady after he had taken care of his uncle. But our Lady surprised him and stood in his path. Frightened, Juan fell to his knees. He told our Lady of his dying uncle, for whom he was rushing to get a priest. Our Lady told him that it was not necessary to go for the priest because his uncle was now perfectly well.

She sent Juan to the top of the hill to gather the roses he would find. Juan knew that there were only bleak rocks up there, but since our Lady had sent him, he trusted her. To his amazement, Juan found beautiful roses swaying in the breeze. He gathered them and placed them in his tilma, a sort of cloak he wore. As happy and as exited as a child, Juan brought them to our Lady, who delicately rearranged the roses in his tilma. She instructed Juan not to show anyone but the bishop what he was carrying.

Juan joyously went to the bishop's palace, knowing that he would be believed. The servants made him wait, but Juan did not mind. They noticed that he was holding something in his tilma. They became curious and wanted to know what treasure he was carrying. Juan told them that what he had was only for the bishop. One servant, more curious that the others, tried to clutch one end of the tilma. He saw a rose and tried to grab it. He grabbed at thin air. The room was suddenly filled with wonderful perfume. When told about it, the bishop immediately sent for Juan. Excited and happy, Juan told the bishop everything that had taken place since his last interview. Then, holding his tilma open, he offered the roses to the bishop. The bishop was surprised to see roses at that time of the year, and such beauties. But what brought the bishop and his attendants to their knees was what they saw on Juan's tilma. Juan was as surprised as the bishop. There on his tilma was the picture of our Lady exactly as Juan had seen her.

The bishop reverently loosened the tilma from Juan's shoulder. He placed the heaven-painted picture in his chapel until the shrine requested by our Lady could be built.

The following day, the bishop went to the hill of Tepeyac with Juan, whom he had kept at the palace. Juan pointed out the different places where our Lady had appeared to him. He then asked permission to go to his uncle, whom our Lady had announced cured. The bishop sent for Bernardino. The old man, strong and vigorous, told the bishop that our Lady had cured him completely and had instructed him to tell the bishop to erect a shrine in which to honor the image, which she wished to be venerated under the title of Our Lady of Guadalupe.

News of the miracles spread very quickly among the Indians as well as the Spaniards. So many people came to see the miraculous tilma that the bishop had to place it in the cathedral for veneration.

At Tepeyac the Indians worked swiftly to build a chapel for our Lady. They would build a shrine later. They wanted something in her honor immediately. Within two weeks the adobe chapel was ready. A great procession took place from the cathedral to Tepeyac, a three-mile trek. The bishop and the town dignitaries, the Franciscan friars, the Spaniards and the Indians all escorted our Lady to her chapel.

The excited Aztecs were in a fiesta mood. For hours they danced to their new Mother. Every now and then, they would stop to hear over and over the story of the miracles. The beautiful Lady loved them; she was their

Mother, she was their Lady. The Indians began to look to our Lady with hope and love. Her miraculous image seemed to radiate the splendors of the true Faith. In a few years the whole of Mexico had become Christian. Countless people were baptized. The churches overflowed with so many converts that in many places Mass was said in the open meadows.

Through the centuries that followed, the temple of Tepeyac grew in size and splendor. Today, it is a massive and beautiful basilica. The great metropolis, Mexico City, has gradually crept up to Tepeyac and surrounded it. Pope Benedict XIV solemnly declared Our Lady of Guadalupe protectress and principal patroness of Mexico.

In 1895, the pious women of Mexico, in gratitude to our Lady, planned to crown the painting. While the ladies were making the plans, getting papal approval, and appealing for jewels, gold and money for the crown, the one on our Lady's head in the picture completely disappeared. Our Lady showed by a miracle that she wanted their gift. A famous jeweler in Paris made the crown, which is a masterpiece. On October 12, 1895, the coronation ceremonies took place with great splendor and festivity. Our Lady was crowned Mexico's Queen. In 1910, Our Lady of Guadalupe was declared patroness of all Latin America, where a great devotion to her had spread. Copies of the miraculous image have received public veneration in many places—Rome, Paris, New Orleans, New Mexico, California, Spain, and especially in South America.

The painting, which is over four hundred years old, is in itself a perpetual miracle, bearing the stamp of the supernatural. Juan's tilma, of coarse fiber, has been wonderfully preserved through the centuries. The picture is as beautiful as when the bishop, kneeling at Juan's feet, beheld the image for the first time. No artist has been able to reproduce the marvelous beauty of this painting. It has been carefully studied and examined. It remains a puzzle to many an artist. Recently, with the aid of a powerful microscope, the reflection of a little man, (Juan) was detected in the pupil of the Lady's eyes.

Mexico has had a turbulent history. Many attempts have been made to destroy the shrine and our Lady's picture. The enemies of the Church try to strike at the heart of Catholic devotion. A bomb planted on our Lady's altar destroyed the alter, crucifix and candlesticks, but the picture remained unharmed.

During Calles' persecution of the Church in the early nineteen hundreds, plans were made to destroy the picture. When the rumors spread, the whole population of Mexico seemed to gather to protect our Lady's shrine. The people of Mexico love our Lady and she loves them.

Impressive to the visitors of Mexico is the realization of just how much our Lady of Guadalupe is part of the very life of the people. She is real to them; she is their mother. Her picture is seen in taxicabs, in buses, in hotels, in homes, in outdoor shrines. The people of Mexico venerate her and love to speak of her.

Throughout the year, pilgrimages are made to her shrine. It is edifying to see the spirit of sacrifice and prayer as so many of the pilgrims make their way to our Lady's shrine on their knees, praying with outstretched arms, love beaming from their upturned faces.

To many of the people of Mexico, Our Lady of Guadalupe is the patroness of North and South America. They feel that our Lady did not come to this continent only for Mexico. She came to bless the Americas, the Western Hemisphere. She should be the acknowledged patroness of all the Americas—North, South and Central, for she is the Mother of all, a powerful pan-American protectress.

XII

Our Lady of Prompt Succor

In 1812 the Vieux Carré with flames was
    overspread,
But a white light overpowered
Those yellow tongues and red,
As strong night wind turned flames back
    flames to fight,
    And saved was the Crescent City.
O Lady of Louisiana,
Your power was that white light
Which saved a charred city from a horrible
    plight.

Three years later on Chalmette's Plains,
    Jackson felt your ray
And solemnly acknowledged heaven's aid
In the victory of the day.
For vanquished were the British—thus his
    vow he did spare—
    And saved was the Crescent City.
O Lady of Prompt Succor,
Your miraculous intervention, resulting from
    prayer,
Proved to a trusting, grateful people your
    tender motherly care.

And now, O patroness of this state, may your
    loving children see
The value that God places in prayer
    addressed to you.
As heavy black clouds loom low, our simple
    trust will bear,
    And saved shall be the Crescent City.
For, O Lady of our Land,
You love to find faithful hearts and heartfelt
    prayer,
And that you can—on the Gulf, on the river,
    on the bayou, in the "ole armchair."

To understand our Lady of Prompt Succor's manifestations of love for Louisiana, and Louisiana's love for Mary, the pages of Louisiana's history must be turned back to its very beginnings, to the days, many years ago, when the people of Europe first began to come to America—to the days of La Salle and Bienville.

La Salle claimed for France all the land drained by the Mississippi River and its tributaries. He called the land Louisiana in honor of the French king and queen Louis XIV and Anne. It was a vast territory, stretching all the way from Canada to the Gulf of Mexico and from the Appalachian Mountains to the Rockies. New Orleans, at the mouth of the Mississippi River, became one of the most important settlements.

Under the wise administration of Bienville, New Orleans soon grew to such an extent that the settlers felt the need of a school for their children. In 1727, a small band of French Ursuline sisters was sent to New Orleans to take charge of the Royal Hospital and to conduct a school. Bienville gave them his house to live in until their convent was built. These Ursulines were the first sisters to come over to what is now the United States. Soon there was a flourishing school for girls and young ladies in New Orleans.

As years passed, the English on the Atlantic coast began to push westward into the land claimed by France. England claimed the Mississippi River Valley also. Through the years, conflicts arose between the two nations. Finally in 1763, as a result of the French and Indian War, France had to give England all her land east of the Mississippi River except New Orleans, which she gave to her ally, Spain, along with all her land west of the Mississippi River. Thereafter, only the territory west of the Mississippi River and New Orleans was called Louisiana.

Since New Orleans was under Spanish rule, no more French Ursulines came to join the sisters stationed there. Instead, Spanish Ursalines were sent to carry on the work.

In 1789, a terrible revolution broke out in France. The French people, overburdened by heavy taxation, no longer wanted a king and queen. They revolted against the nobility, against the Church, against anyone or anything that tried to stop them from getting control of the government. The king, the queen, and many of the nobility were put to death. Churches and convents were destroyed, closed or taken over. Priests and sisters were forced to flee, but many were put to death. It was as though "hell" had broken loose in France. One group of people controlled the government for a while; then another group overpowered them. It meant death for the conquered group. No one felt safe in France.

Finally, one man, with a powerful personality and the backing of the French army, was able to restore order in France. That man was Napoleon Bonaparte. He was very ambitious and dreamed of conquering and ruling the whole world. He began to put his dream into reality by subduing not only France but much of the rest of Europe as well. That meant war, and war is costly.

In 1800, Napoleon made a secret treaty with Spain whereby he received all of Louisiana. He began to dream of a colonial empire in America. But because his European wars meant money and it would be difficult to protect a possession so far away, in 1803 Napoleon decided to sell Louisiana to the United States. The U.S. government had already become aware of the secret treaty and had sent special envoys to France to try to purchase New Orleans by all means, even if they had to offer ten million dollars for it. The control of the mouth of the

Mississippi River had become very important for the welfare of the United States. When Napoleon offered the whole of Louisiana for fifteen million dollars, the astonished and happy American envoys unhesitatingly accepted.

The official transactions for turning Louisiana over to the United States were soon completed. Since the Spanish flag still waved over the territory because of the secrecy of the 1800 treaty, the French flag had to officially replace it. Within twenty days, the stars and the stripes went up as the French flag came down. There had been three different national flags flying over Louisiana in less than a month.

This sudden change caused surprise and consternation among some of the Louisianians. Some rejoiced, some feared, others did not know what to think. The majority of the Ursulines in New Orleans had been Spanish. But before the city's transfer to the United States, fearing for the future, especially under the French flag, sixteen Spanish sisters had left New Orleans for Havanna, Cuba, where they opened a convent and school under the protection of the Spanish king. With more than they could possibly do, the seven remaining Ursulines faced the future with fearful hearts.

The Ursulines did not fear being under the "stars and stripes." When the superior wrote to the president of the United States asking if their property rights would be respected by the new government, President Thomas Jefferson sent the sisters a beautiful, reassuring letter. He told them that under the Constitution and the government of the United States they had a sure guarantee of freedom of worship and of education, that property rights were sacred and that they were free to govern their insti-

tution according to their own rules without fear of inter-
ference from civil authority.

What the Ursulines really feared was that their community would die out if they could get no more sisters
from Europe. They knew of the terrible sufferings of the
Church in France, how the churches and convents had
been destroyed and that their sisters had been scattered
or put to death.

Mother St. André thought of a cousin of hers, also
an Ursuline, Mother St. Michael, who, like many of the
others during the Revolution, had been forced to return
home. In 1802, when things had calmed down, Mother
St. Michael had gone to Montpellier, where, with the
consent of the bishop, she had established a school. She
was trying to do all she could to re-establish her Order in
France. Many young girls had begun to join her. With
growing satisfaction their bishop watched the wonderful
work they were doing in his diocese.

Mother St. André wrote to Mother St. Michael, telling her of their terrible misfortune and how she feared
for the very existence of their Order in New Orleans if
they could get no more sisters. She pleaded for help.
Mother St. Michael did not know what to do. She felt
that she was needed in France, and yet she wanted to
help her sisters in New Orleans. She took her problem to
the bishop of Montpellier. He told her that he needed her
and her workers in his diocese, so he could not let her go.
He added that if she felt that she had to go, the only one
who could grant such a permission would be the Pope.
Now he knew, as did Mother St. Michael, that such
permission was practically impossible to obtain.

Not only was the ambitious Napoleon at war again,
but he also held Pope Pius VII captive at Rome. He had
tried to force the Pope to give him the power of control-

ling and regulating the Catholic Church in France. He had also tried to force the Pope to join him in war against England. When the Pope had refused in both instances, Napoleon, in anger, had had the Pope taken prisoner. Then he had added the Papal States to his own French Empire. While the Pope's jailers were awaiting the transfer of the Pope to Fontainebleu in France, they were obeying strict orders to prevent all communications with the Holy Father.

Mother St. Michael knew this, but she decided to write to the Pope anyway. She promised our Blessed Mother that, if she would obtain a favorable answer, help the sisters get to New Orleans and quickly remove all the obstacles in their way, a statue would be made and devotion spread to Our Lady of Prompt Succor. Prompt succor means "speedy help," and that is just what our Lady gave Mother St. Michael.

In a very short time, Mother St. Michael's prayer was answered in a most remarkable way. She received an agreeable answer from the Pope through his secretary. All the obstacles were removed, and she and her companions were able to join her sisters in New Orleans.

True to her promise, on December 31, 1810, Mother St. Michael placed in the New Orleans convent chapel a precious, newly-carved statue of our Lady, which the Bishop of Montpellier had asked to bless himself. From that time, public honor has been given the Blessed Virgin Mary under the title of Our Lady of Prompt Succor.

In 1812, Louisiana, in its present size, was admitted into the Union as a state. The rest of the large territory eventually became other states. In the same year, a terrible fire broke out in New Orleans. The wind was quickly driving the flames toward the convent. The sisters were told that to remain there any longer was very dangerous, for the fire was out of control. Sister St. Anthony quickly got a small statue of Our Lady of Prompt Succor, which she placed on a window sill facing the raging fire. At the same time, Mother St. Michael fell on her knees, exclaiming, "Our Lady of Prompt Succor, we are lost if you do not help us!" Our Lady heard that prayer! The wind changed and the raging fire died out. The convent was out of danger and the rest of New Orleans had been saved from destruction.

During the same year as the terrible fire, a war broke out between the Americans and the British. It lasted a number of years. In 1815, a famous battle was fought near New Orleans, on the plains of Chalmette. Here again our Lady saved New Orleans.

Andrew Jackson, the American general, had six thousand men to fight against fifteen thousand trained British soldiers. A hopeless situation for the Americans! Jackson vowed that if the Americans lost the battle, the British would find New Orleans in a heap of ruins because he would fight to the end. He would not let them take the city.

The sisters spent the night of January seventh in prayer before the Blessed Sacrament. The chapel was filled with devout ladies and girls, all weeping and praying at the foot of the holy statue. Our Lady was listening to the prayers of her children and was pleading their cause with her divine Son.

On the morning of January 8, 1815, holy Mass was offered in the presence of the statue of Our Lady of Prompt Succor. The thundering of the cannons and guns could be distinctly heard by all in the chapel. Just before Mass began, the superior, in the name of the community, made a vow to have a Mass of Thanksgiving sung every year should the Americans be victorious. At Communion time, a messenger rushed into the chapel to announce the joyful news of an American victory. Our Lady had again saved New Orleans.

Surprised by the readiness of the American line and the steady firing from the Americans, the English had been thrown into confusion and disorder. In twenty-five minutes it was almost all over. The English lost over 2,600 men on the battlefield while, according to some historical records, only six Americans died and seven were wounded. The rest of the English had quickly retreated. Such a victory was really a miracle.

Jackson, the great hero of the day, did not hesitate to admit that he had received marvelous help from heaven. He asked the vicar general, William Dubourg, to have a service of public thanksgiving performed in the cathedral. On January twenty-third, a solemn high Mass of thanksgiving was celebrated in St. Louis Cathedral by Father Dubourg, who later became bishop of New Orleans. General Jackson and his staff visited the Ursuline sisters to thank them personally for the prayers which had helped him gain so brilliant a victory.

Today, January eighth is observed as the anniversary of the Battle of New Orleans, but it is also the anniversary of the day on which the city was saved from destruction through the intercession of Our Lady of Prompt Succor.

The first shrine of Our Lady of Prompt Succor was on Chartres Street in the first Ursuline convent, which was completed in 1734 under the supervision of Bienville. It is the most ancient landmark in the city of New Orleans today and is considered the oldest building in the Mississippi valley. It was to that convent that Mother St. Michael brought her statue in 1810. It was there that Father Dubourg offered the holy sacrifice of the Mass for the success of the American Army on January 8, 1815, and the Ursuline sisters made the vow to have a solemn high Mass celebrated annually on the anniversary of the Battle of New Orleans.

In 1824, the miraculous statue was taken to a second shrine in the new home of the Ursulines on 4580 Dauphine Street. It was in this chapel that the solemn coronation of the miraculous statue took place.

Archbishop Francis Janssens, a devoted lover of our Lady, knowing of the countless streams of blessings and graces she had let flow over New Orleans since 1810, longed to see our Lady's famed statue liturgically crowned. In 1894, on one of his official visits to Rome, he presented a petition from the Ursuline sisters to the Holy Father, adding his own recommendations for the solemn coronation. Not only did he receive pontifical approval but he was designated to crown our Lady's statue in the Pope's name. November 10, 1895, was set as the day for the ceremonies.

The people of New Orleans and the surrounding towns were so generous with their donations of precious jewels, rings and pins, necklaces and bracelets, that two magnificent crowns were made, one for our Lady and one for the Infant Jesus. A solemn novena preceded the coronation ceremonies. As the delegate of the Holy Father, Pope Leo XIII, Archbishop Janssens joyfully blessed the two crowns, read the papal decree ordering the coronation, and then placed the crowns upon the heads of Mary and her Child. A solemn Pontifical Mass followed the impressive ceremony. Archbishop Janssens then consecrated everyone to the great Mother of God and begged all to be faithful in their service to her divine Son until death would call them to his kingdom.

Archbishop Janssens did not realize that his own call would come so soon; nor did he dream that our Lady would openly manifest her own love for her devoted son. Two years later, in June 1897, he set sail for France on financial business. As his ship, the *Creole*, skirted the banks of the Mississippi, the Archbishop's eyes lighted up as they passed the Ursuline chapel. The chancellor, Father Thibault, noted that the Archbishop looked exceptionally tired.

Gradually the land began to disappear. Suddenly the Archbishop was gripped by a severe pain in his chest. Father Thibault helped him to his room. The Archbishop tried to calm Father's fears by telling him that he would be all right. Early the next morning, after receiving the Anointing of the Sick from his chancellor, the Archbishop breathed his last.

Poor Father Thibault was in great distress. He felt he had to get his Archbishop's body back to New Orleans. The ship's captain refused to turn back to new Orleans for "the sake of a dead man." He said his passengers had rights upon which he could not infringe, and the only thing that Father could do was to bury the body at sea, since no other ship was due on that particular route for seven days.

When the captain asked the time wished for the burial, Father Thibault answered that he could not see his Archbishop's body thrown into the sea; he felt responsible for him and he had to see that the people of New Orleans would receive the body of their beloved Archbishop to give it a proper burial. He asked to be given one hour and to be left alone. The captain left the priest.

Father Thibault immediately fell on his knees and passionately pleaded with Our Lady of Prompt Succor to come to his assistance. He promised that if she would send a ship on its way to New Orleans within the hour that he would say fifty Masses of thanksgiving in her honor. He promised to say nine of the Masses in the Ursuline convent before her miraculous statue. Father continued to pray beside the body of his beloved Archbishop.

Suddenly the captain rushed in excitedly, saying that a ship had been sighted heading for New Orleans. It was being signaled to stop so Father Thibault could prepare to board it. With a grateful heart, Father Thibault made preparations for the transfer of the body to the *Hudson* which was anchored about a quarter of a mile from the *Creole*. As the launch carrying the Archbishop's body headed for the *Hudson*, a beautiful rainbow suddenly appeared over the sea, joining the two ships. The sailors and all who beheld the rainbow marveled at its beauty and its position. It was truly a remarkable sign of our Lady's love for the Archbishop and an answer to a cry for help.

Father Thibault readily obtained permission to say his nine promised Masses before our Lady's miraculous statue in the Ursuline chapel. The sisters were as grateful to our Lady as he was.

Our Lady's statue remained in the chapel on Dauphine Street for about one hundred years. But the mighty Mississippi River, with its swift current flowing into the gulf, had been gradually eating into the land. Since the river had swallowed up some of the front lawn of the convent, it soon became necessary for the sisters to find another home. The sisters sold their property on Dauphine Street to the state of Louisiana in 1918.

In solemn procession on December 30, 1923, our Lady—the same wooden carved statue now covered with sparkling gold leaf—was carried to her beautiful votive shrine on State Street. The shrine is a magnificent monument of Christian art.

Each year on January eighth, a solemn high Mass of thanksgiving is sung at the shrine, and as long as Louisiana is Louisiana, New Orleans is New Orleans, and the Ursulines are Ursulines, this vow will be kept.

Many churches in Louisiana bear the name "Our Lady of Prompt Succor" in honor of Mary. For example, the name is found in Alexandria, in Mansura, in Sulphur, in Westwego, in Chalmette, in White Castle, in Chackbay, and in Coteau.

Statues and pictures of Our Lady of Prompt Succor can be found in many other churches, convents and homes. In the Jesuit church on Baronne Street, Immaculate Conception, there is a large, beautiful mosaic of Our Lady of Prompt Succor. At the bottom of the picture are two smaller pictures: one, New Orleans in flames; and the other, the fighting flames of Chalmette. This mosaic is exceptionally beautiful in color, design and workmanship. Our Lady of Prompt Succor in her pink dress and blue mantle is almost life-size and seems to radiate blessings upon New Orleans.

Our Lady of Prompt Succor loves Louisiana. She still has many blessings to pour down upon her children, but she does want to be asked for them. Devotion, love and imitation will obtain countless blessings upon Louisiana, from Louisiana's patroness, Our Lady of Prompt Succor.

BOOKS & MEDIA

The Daughters of St. Paul operate book and media centers at the following addresses. Visit, call or write the one nearest you today, or find us on the World Wide Web, www.pauline.org.

CALIFORNIA
3908 Sepulveda Blvd., Culver City, CA 90230; 310-397-8676
5945 Balboa Ave., San Diego, CA 92111; 619-565-9181
46 Geary Street, San Francisco, CA 94108; 415-781-5180

FLORIDA
145 S.W. 107th Ave., Miami, FL 33174; 305-559-6715

HAWAII
1143 Bishop Street, Honolulu, HI 96813; 808-521-2731

ILLINOIS
172 North Michigan Ave., Chicago, IL 60601; 312-346-4228

LOUISIANA
4403 Veterans Memorial Blvd., Metairie, LA 70006; 504-887-7631

MASSACHUSETTS
Rte. 1, 885 Providence Hwy., Dedham, MA 02026; 781-326-5385

MISSOURI
9804 Watson Rd., St. Louis, MO 63126; 314-965-3512

NEW JERSEY
561 U.S. Route 1, Wick Plaza, Edison, NJ 08817; 732-572-1200

NEW YORK
150 East 52nd Street, New York, NY 10022; 212-754-1110
78 Fort Place, Staten Island, NY 10301; 718-447-5071

OHIO
2105 Ontario Street, Cleveland, OH 44115; 216-621-9427

PENNSYLVANIA
9171-A Roosevelt Blvd., Philadelphia, PA 19114; 215-676-9494

SOUTH CAROLINA
243 King Street, Charleston, SC 29401; 803-577-0175

TENNESSEE
4811 Poplar Ave., Memphis, TN 38117; 901-761-2987

TEXAS
114 Main Plaza, San Antonio, TX 78205; 210-224-8101

VIRGINIA
1025 King Street, Alexandria, VA 22314; 703-549-3806

CANADA
3022 Dufferin Street, Toronto, Ontario, Canada M6B 3T5; 416-781-9131
1155 Yonge Street, Toronto, Ontario, Canada M4T 1W2; 416-934-3440

¡Libros en español!